Witch's Brew

Witch's Brew

MAGICKAL COCKTAILS
TO RAISE
THE SPIRITS

SHAWN ENGELS

STEVEN NICHOLS

STERLING EPICURE
New York

STERLING EPICURE
New York

ISBN: 978-1-4549-4286-3 (print format)
ISBN: 978-1-4549-4386-0 (e-book)

Distributed in Canada by Sterling Publishing Co., Inc.
c/o Canadian Manda Group, 664 Annette Street
Toronto, Ontario M6S 2C8, Canada
Distributed in the United Kingdom by GMC Distribution Services
Castle Place, 166 High Street, Lewes, East Sussex BN7 1XU, England
Distributed in Australia by NewSouth Books
University of New South Wales, Sydney, NSW 2052, Australia

For information about custom editions, special sales,
and premium and corporate purchases, please contact
Sterling Special Sales at 800-805-5489
or specialsales@sterlingpublishing.com.

Manufactured in Singapore

2 4 6 8 10 9 7 5 3 1

sterlingpublishing.com
Cover design by Elizabeth Mihaltse Lindy
Interior design by Christine Heun

Photo Credits
All photographs by Rachel Johnson, except:
Getty Images: DigitalVision Vectors: 4khz: 122; whitemay: 10;
iStock/Getty Images Plus: v_zaitsev: throughout (smoke)
Shutterstock.com: mmalkani: throughout (decorative print);
Lunov Mykola: 8; Nimaxs: 6

Table of Contents

WITCHCRAFT

AH, WITCHCRAFT. THE TERM CONJURES IMAGES of green-faced, dowdy women with stringy hair and menacing cackles. Their presence makes pious mortals tremble with anxiety for fear of being hexed, cursed, and bound.

Witchcraft has had a glow up as of late, however. Our society has been changing rapidly, and its reliance on social media has ushered in a newfound transparency when it comes to lifestyle, along with the ability to connect folks all over the world. Because of the widespread ability to connect with people who feel the same way we do, witches are coming out of the broom closet left and right. Personally, I love witchcraft for many reasons, but the biggest reason is because it is an art form and a practice tailored to each practitioner.

So what exactly defines witchcraft as we understand it today? In short, witchcraft is the immersion of energy and intention into a desire. Your desire can be as simple as pouring your morning coffee or as complex as bringing love into your life. You have the ability to decide when daily practice becomes witchcraft.

Anyone, anywhere, can be a witch. There is no bloodline that determines whether you are a witch. There are closed religions that are aligned with witchcraft in which there is a culture and ancestry. However, in the eclectic environment that has drawn the attention of many contemporary witches, the only requirement for entry is a desire to learn and read anything and everything you can.

Because all elements of life are made up of energy, there are also certain intentions that can be paired with each energetic vibration in our universe. So on every path a witch decides to walk, they can amplify their own daily intentions by creating a ripe energetic environment with a variety of ingredients. This can be created by using crystals, herbs, candles, colors, and more!

For example, if a witch has the intention to protect herself, she can use a crystal to do that. Obsidian can ward off negative energy, but the same effect can be produced by using an herb like basil, a black candle, or a mixture of the three. These physical ingredients can also be paired with a repetitive mantra, or incantation, and lo and behold, you have designed an entire spell.

I like to teach witches how to find magick in the mundane, because when you start living with magick in mind, you begin to live more intentionally, and then more abundantly—which is where the art of cocktailing comes in. Creating a drink to enjoy by yourself or with others is already such an artistic and energetically joyous experience that, when combined with an intention and the knowledge of what you're actually creating, you can elevate the magick!

In using this book, you will see how crafting a cocktail can be a ritualistic experience and how imbibing can raise your energetic vibration. In no time, you'll be firming up your relationship with cocktailing, moving from simply drinking what tastes good to crafting an intentional potion.

HERBOLOGY AND ELIXIRS

As stated in the previous section, there are certain intentions attributed to the energy of objects like plants—basil protects, rosemary wards off sickness and nightmares, sage cleanses. Many witches, especially those deemed "Kitchen Witches" (those that are most comfortable creating their magick in the kitchen), practice herbology, the study of plants. By researching different types and strains of plants, you can determine which spells they can best support.

Herbs have tons of different correlations. Some are said to have masculine energy, which would be best for spells requiring action, aggression, or

determination. Those that are said to be feminine would be best for creation, manifestation, fertility, or intuition. There are also planetary correspondences, alignments with certain deities, and medicinal properties that all make up the nature of a plant. You will see how this works, in depth, in the contents of this book.

If you think of many family remedies based off of "old wives' tales," you can break apart each ingredient to find its magickal correspondence. All of these recipes, passed down through generations, are based on folk magick, which is also called hearth magick. For example, one of the most common cold remedies, tea with honey and lemon, can be understood in a magickal sense by looking at all of the components individually. Black tea has caffeine, which is known to eliminate grogginess. Honey is known to soothe the throat. And lemon is said to break down mucus. But further? Black tea leaves are medicinally anti-inflammatory and highly oxidized, which makes them great for banishment. Honey boosts energy, aids in digestion, and prevents certain bacteria from growing, so it's no wonder it is used in many healing spells. Lemon is very high in vitamin C and is known to prevent asthma, cancer, and strokes. Energetically, this fruit is used for cleansing spells (and even as a household cleaner in practical magick!).

So how does this work with cocktailing? Is it wise to work magick while under the influence? How do we heal while simultaneously indulging in a vice? The answers to these questions lie in the overall purpose of the act.

Sometimes the best self-care we can perform is tuning out. And for eons, humans have been using altered states to do this. As far as tuning in? You can also use an altered state to tap into the spirit realm, connecting with energies that may be otherwise inaccessible. Alcohol can be a very potent tool, and when using it with respect, you can unlock a new level of partaking. When we responsibly satisfy a desire that is backed by an intention, we make the act a truly magickal practice.

THE RITUAL OF IMBIBING: A HISTORY

ONE OF THE MOST RECOGNIZABLE MANIFESTATIONS OF THE act of "tying one on" is the Greek god Dionysus, who rules over wine, pleasure, festivity, and even madness. Dionysus, like many Greek deities, had an extremely traumatic childhood. This began with Hera, the wife of Zeus, causing the death of his mother by persuading her to ask Zeus to reveal himself to her while she was pregnant, in all of his godlike glory. The lightning bolts springing from Zeus's body killed her, and Dionysus was taken into Zeus's thigh to be born. Madness followed Dionysus pretty much everywhere he went, with the jealous Hera thrusting his caregivers and even Dionysus himself into madness at many points throughout his journey. But during his childhood, in order to keep him safe from Hera, Dionysus was brought up as a girl and taught the art of the vine, making him a creator. As an outcast, he was dubbed Eleutherios, or "the liberator," by his followers because his use of wine, music, and frenzy freed them from social restraints and self-consciousness.

Christianity has quite deep roots when it comes to booze. Wine symbolizes the blood of Christ and is used in many ceremonies, such as Holy Communion. In European Christianity, alcohol is also used,—like grappa in Italy and and Greece, and vodka in Eastern Russian traditions. Tequila and mezcal are used in Mexico to celebrate certain occasions, such as Easter or at funerals. The use of alcohol in religious ceremonies has always been very sacramental, whether the intention is to take part in tradition or free yourself from conventional norms, as with the followers of Dionysus. As long as we have an intention present, alcohol contains a ritual purpose.

Hooch is also widely known as an offering to deities. A spirit for a spirit, if you will. Many traditions recommend leaving out a shot of the liquor of choice for one of your grandparents before asking them for guidance. In some closed religions, such as Vodou or Santeria, rum or tequila is used as an offering to certain Loa in order to carry out a spell. Wine and whiskey are excellent gifts for most deities, but it is wise to research what they like before asking for their help. It's like buying your friend a bottle of white when they really prefer red—if you don't take the time to get to know their preference, will they help you out with a favor? For example, my matron goddess Freyja enjoys mead, so I leave out a glass for her every Friday, her day. Taking a sip of your offering is also seen as a sacrifice in some instances and can help you connect with your spirit of choice.

If you don't drink alcohol, this book is still for you! You can still do all of the ritualistic practices, make offerings to your deities, and even change your conscious state. All of the drinks and rituals in this book can be modified to fit an alcohol-abstained lifestyle. By using the main ingredients in each of the cocktails and pairing them with soda water instead of the spirit in the recipe, you will still infuse their energetic properties into your concoction. Plus, meditation on its own can lead to an effectively altered state with which to carry out your intention. Whether you drink responsibly or don't drink at all, these recipes will have you experiencing the effects of a magickal potion in no time.

The
Goddess

DIVINE FEMININE ENERGY IS THE SOURCE OF creation. Without a womb, there would be no birth. Without Mother Earth, there would be no growth. Without intuition, creation would not be protected. Goddess energy is known throughout pantheons to invoke energies ranging from sensual to warlike, but with all the underlying spirit of protection, fertility, and wisdom. Neo-pagan practitioners have categorized goddesses into four kinds: the maiden, the mother, the crone, and the triple goddess. All will take you through the energetic life cycles of divine feminine energy. The cocktails in this section will connect you directly to this vibration as you indulge.

THE MAIDEN

ONE OF THE THREE GENERATIONS OF THE GODDESS, THE maiden symbolizes purity and fertility. The Greek goddess of the underworld, Persephone, embodies this sentiment, but with a dark twist. As a young maiden picking flowers in an open field, Persephone was seen by Hades, lord of the underworld, and stolen away on his chariot to rule alongside him. Demeter, her mother, heartbroken and determined to find her, went looking for Persephone. Upon learning where she was, Hades gave in and prepared to take Persephone back. But before he did, he offered Persephone a pomegranate to satiate her, as she had been on a hunger strike since her abduction. As a last ruse, the six pomegranate seeds that she ate bound her to the underworld for six months out of the year, but each spring, she would return to the earth and bring the bloom with her.

Pomegranate has long been associated with fertility. As a fruit comprised of mostly juicy seeds, it is a feminine plant corresponding to creation. Its bloodred color correlates to passion and romance, and its hard outer shell, which protects the succulent seeds within, makes it a fruit with strong ties to strength and resilience.

When preparing this cocktail, invoke Persephone and drink down the duality of her nature. Before you begin mixing, ground yourself and sink into meditation, first envisioning the bloom of spring and then the dead of winter. Imagine the cycles of the seasons as you mix and the energy being poured into your cocktail. As you sip, imagine the bloom of spring again, each flower petal unfolding into your mouth as you bring to life the maiden goddess.

→ → →

THE MAIDEN

MOON PHASE: Waxing moon
OCCASION: Spring, Ostara (spring equinox), bridal shower
GLASSWARE: High ball

INGREDIENTS

1½ oz tequila blanco
½ oz pomegranate liqueur
1 oz mango juice
½ oz lime juice
½ oz simple syrup
Pomegranate seeds

DIRECTIONS

* Build the tequila, pomegranate liqueur, mango juice, lime juice, and simple syrup in a shaker with ice.

* Shake vigorously.

* Strain into a glass with ice.

* Top with pomegranate seeds for garnish.

NONALCOHOLIC MODIFICATION

* Substitute pomegranate liqueur with pomegranate juice.

* Build 1.5 oz pomegranate juice, 1.5 oz mango juice, lime juice, and simple syrup in a shaker with ice.

* Shake vigorously.

* Strain into a glass with ice.

* Top with pomegranate seeds for garnish.

THE
MOTHER

THE SECOND OF THE GODDESS GENERATION LIES IN THE mother. While the maiden is fertile and pure, the mother is a creator. She has life within her and is a fierce protector. By giving birth, an incredibly magickal act, she has generated a life that she is, instinctually, sworn to guard and care for against all other duties. So in this, the mother represents the ability to generate life and the strength to protect it. While this seems like a very exclusive right, we can invoke the power of motherhood no matter who we are. We can create art, businesses, and meals. We can nurture plants, animals, and ourselves. We can protect our friends, family, and home. The might of the mother can enrich us all.

Apples are connected with goddesses for many reasons, in addition to their associations with fertility. When cut in half, you will see that the seeds are arranged in a pentagram, symbolizing all of the elements made within the womb of the fruit. Linked to mother goddesses like Demeter and Hera, the apple also indicates a wisdom only attained through motherhood. Also the symbol of teaching, it shows the nurturing side of education.

As you prepare this cocktail, dream about what you wish to create. What would you like to birth into existence? While mixing this drink, meditate on what you want to manifest and keep it strong in your mind's eye. As you drink down this cocktail, with every sip, ask for the wisdom and magick to make it so.

→ → →

THE MOTHER

MOON PHASE: Full moon
OCCASION: Spring, Beltane, baby shower
GLASSWARE: High ball

INGREDIENTS

1½ oz rye whiskey
1½ oz apple cider
½ oz lemon juice
½ oz vanilla citrus liqueur
Apple sliced horizontally across equator

DIRECTIONS

* Build the rye whiskey, apple cider, lemon juice, and vanilla citrus liqueur in a shaker with ice.

* Shake vigorously.

* Strain into a glass with ice.

* Top with apple slice for garnish.

NONALCOHOLIC MODIFICATION

* Substitute vanilla citrus liqueur with vanilla simple syrup.

* Build 3 oz of apple cider, lemon juice, and vanilla simple syrup in a shaker with ice.

* Shake vigorously.

* Strain into a glass with ice.

* Top with apple slice for garnish.

THE TRIPLE GODDESS

Finally, the triple goddess is the embodiment of all three generations. Containing the fertility and purity of the maiden, the creativity and sexuality of the mother, and the wisdom of the crone, the triple goddess is a force to be reckoned with. The goddess Hecate is an example of a triple goddess, as she rules the heavens, the earth, and the underworld. She is often depicted as the phases of the moon, with a waxing crescent as the maiden, a full moon as the mother, and a waning crescent as the crone. The life cycle of the goddess follows monthly lunations, beginning again every 29.5 days.

In order to do the triple goddess justice, there must be three pivotal ingredients to invoke the proper energy for her presence. Peach, a ripe and juicy fruit with a large pit, is energetically linked to the maiden. Secreting a deep-red color and being a lesser-known aphrodisiac, hibiscus correlates to the formative and sensual nature of the mother and also the passion it takes to protect. Another use of aged liquor, this time rum, symbolizes the crone to tie this cocktail all together.

In mixing this cocktail, invoke each element of the goddess separately when adding in their respective ingredient. As you add in the peach, ask for undiluted judgement. Add the hibiscus and ask for the ability to conceive in your own perfect way. Add the aged liquor and ask for the wisdom you'll need to guide you. And as you sip your cocktail, surrender to the process and let the ideas the triple goddess has inspired flood your mind.

THE TRIPLE GODDESS

MOON PHASE: New moon
OCCASION: Birthdays, promotions, new projects
GLASSWARE: High ball

INGREDIENTS

  1½ oz aged rum
  1 oz peach nectar
  1½ oz chilled green tea
  ½ oz Demerara syrup
  ½ oz lemon juice
  ½ oz hibiscus syrup
  Edible flower for garnish

DIRECTIONS

* Build the rum, peach nectar, green tea, Demerara syrup, and lemon juice in a shaker with ice.

* Shake vigorously.

* Pour hibiscus syrup into a glass filled with ice.

* Top with the contents of the shaker to layer.

* Add an edible flower for garnish.

NONALCOHOLIC MODIFICATION

* Build the peach nectar, 3 oz of green tea, Demerara syrup, and lemon juice in a shaker with ice.

* Shake vigorously.

* Pour hibiscus syrup into a glass filled with ice.

* Top with the contents of the shaker to layer.

* Add an edible flower for garnish.

THE CRONE

THE CRONE TAKES THE WISDOM OF THE MOTHER TO A whole new level! This aged woman has magick in the folds of her skin and the grey of her hair. She has lived life and has learned lessons that only come from experiencing life fully. She symbolizes death and the end of a cycle, but in a way that should be accepted rather than feared. Because of the quality of her life due to her rich and full existence, the end is welcomed. She brings rebirth and transition, as she knows that nothing is truly over. Rather, it changes forms and evolves to fit the current environment.

Because age and wisdom are the name of the game for the crone, I've chosen both bourbon whiskey and elderberry as the star players in this drink. When a whiskey ages, it spends time in a barrel, and where the harsh elements of the alcohol fade, its taste is influenced by the state of its containment. Elderberries are known to bridge the divide between the physical and spirit realms, providing gateways to the underworld. This is much like the life of the crone, who has been matured and molded by life. Having served her purpose, the crone prepares to be reborn again—in this case, as a magickal elixir to be enjoyed by you!

As you create this cocktail, list everything you have in this life to be grateful for. You should even include hardships that you have experienced, for they have brought you to this moment. As you mix, for each ingredient added, name at least one thing that you can thank for bringing you right here, right now. As you sip this concoction, ask for the wisdom to release what no longer serves you, invoking the wisdom of the crone with each taste.

→ → →

THE CRONE

MOON PHASE: Waning moon
OCCASION: Winter, Yule, birthdays
GLASSWARE: Rocks glass

INGREDIENTS

    2 lemon wedges
    4 mint leaves
    1 tsp elderberries
    ¾ oz simple syrup
    2 oz bourbon whiskey
    Lemon wheel
    Additional elderberries for garnish

DIRECTIONS

* Place the lemon wedges, mint leaves, and elderberries in a shaker.

* Muddle well.

* Top with simple syrup, bourbon, and ice.

* Shake vigorously.

* Double strain into a glass with ice.

* Top with lemon wheel and elderberries for garnish.

NONALCOHOLIC MODIFICATION

* Substitute bourbon with iced black tea.

* Place the lemon wedges, mint leaves, and elderberries in a shaker.

* Muddle well.

* Top with simple syrup, tea, and ice.

* Shake vigorously.

* Double strain into a glass with ice.

* Top with lemon wheel and elderberries for garnish.

The Elements

IN WITCHCRAFT, IT IS SAID THAT EVERYTHING is influenced by the elements. Whether it's the grounding nature of the earth, the quick pace of wind, the destructive force of fire, the motion of water, or the universal guidance of spirit, you can always find at least one energy in any given piece of nature. If you've ever seen a pentacle, which in popular culture is often erroneously connected to evil, you've seen the symbolic representation of the elements. Each point of the five-pointed star represents one of these five influences, which are all bridged together to form one symbol. This is the way that the elements connect us all.

DEPTHS
OF THE OCEAN

THE ELEMENT OF WATER IS SAID TO INFLUENCE DEEP emotions and intuition. Feminine in nature, it has the strength to completely overpower us, as in a tsunami or flood, but can also gently rock us into a nurtured sleep, much like the waves of the ocean. As the calming flow of a stream, it symbolizes the change of the tides, which can influence the earth over long periods of time. To experience water is to deeply feel, rather than to intellectualize. In this, water can also bridge the gap between the human and spirit worlds.

Because it is found in the sea itself, seaweed has a direct connection to the element of water. Seaweed is naturally salty, much like our tears, which allow us to experience the moving quality of intense feelings. Seaweed is often found washed ashore, journeying from the deepest waters to the shallow waves of a beach. While mixing this cocktail, imagine crashing waves, running streams, and falling rain. In whatever way water comes to you, imagine it as it all cycles back to one place, hydrating the earth and evaporating back into the clouds. As you sip your cocktail, imagine the flow of water filling you up, allowing you to access your emotions in ways you never thought possible. Imagine it cleansing you and washing away your worries.

→ → →

DEPTHS OF THE OCEAN

MOON PHASE: Full moon

OCCASION: Breakups, funerals, job relocation

GLASSWARE: Rocks glass

INGREDIENTS

2 oz nori-infused scotch (recipe below)

Islay scotch, for rinse

1 oz lemon juice

1 oz honey syrup

¼ oz ginger liqueur

Additional nori seaweed for garnish

DIRECTIONS FOR NORI-INFUSED SCOTCH

* Infuse two pieces of nori seaweed in one cup of scotch for 2 hours.

DIRECTIONS

* Rinse glass with Islay scotch.
* Combine nori-infused scotch, lemon juice, honey syrup (boil water and mix a 1:1 ratio of honey to hot water), ginger liqueur, and ice into a martini shaker.
* Shake vigorously.
* Hard strain into glass over whiskey cube.
* Finish with nori seaweed garnish.

NONALCOHOLIC MODIFICATION

* Replace scotch with black tea and infuse seaweed per instructions.
* Combine nori-infused tea, lemon juice, honey syrup, ginger bitters, and ice into a martini shaker.
* Shake vigorously.
* Hard strain into glass over whiskey cube.
* Finish with nori seaweed garnish.

FLAMES OF THE SUN

FIRE IS BOTH A CREATOR AND A DESTROYER. THE UNQUENCH-able heat of passion can help create the most incredible art, while even the smallest flame of a match can destroy entire regions. The light of fire also casts a shadow. When using fire, we summon the masculine energy of determination and fertilization that enables us to take action and realize the dreams we have conjured. We must beware, however, because fire can burn us when not controlled.

Ruled by fire, the spicy habanero pepper adds a dose of quick-acting magic. This pepper is also used to remove evil spirits as a cleansing practice. Its flavor adds passion and heat. Pineapple, the accompanying flavor, is both sun-ruled and masculine. Energetically linked to wealth, good fortune, and luck, the pineapple is also the symbol of hospitality. Used in magick to bring people together and bask in abundance, the pineapple is as powerful as it is sweet.

As you mix this cocktail, think of the flames of the sun warming your shoulders and nourishing your body with vitamin D. Imagine fires raging on the top of that large star in the distance, warming up Mother Earth so that she can grow life. As you sip your cocktail, with each tingling of spice, imagine your body filling up with the confidence and the tenacity to conquer all of your desires.

→ → →

FLAMES OF THE SUN

MOON PHASE: Any, best for daytime
OCCASION: Summer, BBQ, new projects, creative projects
GLASSWARE: Rocks glass

INGREDIENTS

1 habanero ring
½ oz lime juice
1½ oz tequila blanco
½ oz chili liqueur
1½ oz pineapple juice
½ oz simple syrup
Habanero for garnish

DIRECTIONS

* Toss the habanero ring and lime juice into a shaker and muddle well.

* Build tequila, chili liqueur, pineapple juice, simple syrup, and ice into the shaker.

* Shake vigorously.

* Double strain into a glass with ice.

* Top with habanero for garnish.

NONALCOHOLIC MODIFICATION

* Toss three habanero rings and lime juice into a shaker and muddle well.

* Build 3 oz of pineapple juice, simple syrup, and ice into the shaker.

* Shake vigorously.

* Double strain into a glass with ice.

* Top with habanero for garnish.

WINDS OF CHANGE

THE ELEMENT OF AIR SYMBOLIZES SWIFT CHANGE, WIT, and intellect. You can invoke air simply by taking in a deep and intentional breath, or by speaking your mind. Just as a tornado can blow down a house or a cool breeze can bring relief on a hot day, your words can and do have impact. Also said to be masculine in nature, air is more action-based than life-giving. We can utilize the divine masculine in this element to set goals into forward motion. It is advised that we use and respect our words just as we do the wind, knowing that it is equally capable of whirling us into a perfect moment or blowing away what no longer serves us.

Associated with the air element, lemongrass is ruled by Mercury, the communication planet. It is great for mental agility and even helps stimulate memory. Used as a study aid, lemongrass can help awaken your mind's capacity to help you speak from a more intentional place. It is also very cleansing, much like the wind, so it will blow away any negativity as you concoct your words of choice.

When mixing this cocktail, imagine a soft breeze turning into roaring winds and creating a billowing motion in your mind strong enough to topple over large structures. As you encounter this natural occurrence and its huge impact, slowly imagine changing the winds your mind created from chaotic to orderly by visualizing them beginning to swirl in a clockwise direction. Imagine the wind blowing away all that doesn't serve you and bringing in all that does directly into the eye of the tornado. As you sip this cocktail, let the wind clear away the clutter in your mind so that you may speak with more direction.

WINDS OF CHANGE

MOON PHASE: Waxing moon
OCCASION: Networking events, business meetings, after study sessions
GLASSWARE: Mug

INGREDIENTS

Tea bag with Earl Grey and
dried lemongrass (3:1 ratio)
1½ oz bourbon
1 packet of Sugar in the Raw®
1 oz coconut milk
2 dashes Angostura bitters
Lemongrass for garnish

DIRECTIONS

* Brew tea in a mug about halfway
  filled with hot water.
* Add bourbon and Sugar in the
  Raw®.
* Top with coconut milk and two
  dashes of bitters.
* Stir.
* Add lemongrass for garnish.

NONALCOHOLIC MODIFICATION

* Brew tea in a mug fully filled
  with hot water.
* Add Sugar in the Raw®.
* Top with coconut milk and two
  dashes of bitters.
* Stir.
* Add lemongrass for garnish.

ROOTS OF THE EARTH

THE EARTH IS A MOTHER BECAUSE EVERYTHING WE KNOW grows from her. She is a life giver, and for that she is feminine and strong. When witches speak of grounding, we are referring to coming into her, associating our energy with the literal ground beneath our feet so we don't fly up into the clouds, as we so often do when we are lost in thought. When plants grow, they are grounded, with roots that curl and twist into fertile soil. As a solid structure that serves as both a container and a source of being, the earth is a heavy and complex formation. However, water can erode it, fire can scorch it, wind can move it, and it can even work against itself, with shifting tectonic plates that can cause an earthquake. Even when grounded, we are reminded to be flexible so that we can evolve.

Carrots as a root vegetable are kin with the soil of the earth. As carrots are known to be good for eyesight, this carrot-infused drink will make you see clearly in a situation that might otherwise be cluttered with emotion. Grounding is best practiced regularly in witchcraft, but it is especially helpful when emotions or the mind are in danger of overtaking the body and blunting intuition. Carrots are particularly powerful in dispelling illusions and creating fertile ground in which our minds can grow. This ingredient will help you to view your situations objectively.

As you mix this cocktail, imagine roots growing from the soles of your feet where you are standing, directly into the core of the earth. Imagine them rooting you into the ground, keeping you level and secure. Imagine them allowing you the ability to walk with just enough slack that you can move about the earth as you desire. As you drink this cocktail, imagine coming into your body with each sip and feeling the earthiness of the flavor profile. Scan your body and notice where you are holding tension. Release it as you enjoy your concoction.

ROOTS OF THE EARTH

MOON PHASE: Any
OCCASION: Funerals, breakups, job relocation
GLASSWARE: Coupette

INGREDIENTS

2 oz mezcal
2 dashes ginger bitters
¾ oz maple syrup
1 oz carrot juice
¾ oz lemon juice
Carrot top for garnish

DIRECTIONS

* Build mezcal, bitters, maple syrup, carrot juice, lemon juice, and ice into a shaker.
* Shake vigorously.
* Strain into the coupette.
* Top with carrot for garnish.

NONALCOHOLIC MODIFICATION

* Substitute mezcal with ginger tea.
* Build 1½ oz ginger tea, 1½ oz carrot juice, maple syrup, lemon juice, and ice into a shaker.
* Shake vigorously.
* Strain into the coupette.
* Top with carrot for garnish.

INVOKING SPIRIT

AND HERE WE ARRIVE AT THE ELEMENT THAT TIES IT ALL together: spirit. The connecting force that brings life into all otherwise-compartmentalized forces. It makes fire hot, wind blow, waves crash, and the earth fertile. It is the undefined, transcendent energy that gives every being purpose. That gives humans the consciousness to taste its existence. It is mystical, glorious, and supreme. It's like a supernatural electricity. And it lives within us all.

Because there is no true way to capture spirit in a glass, I wanted to design a cocktail that was spirit forward, with your intention as the main ingredient. In this, you are the magickal life force that makes this cocktail connect you with the great beyond. Its strength will open you up to a new state of consciousness, and its translucence will elevate your ability to be the perfect vessel for spirit to shine through.

While mixing this cocktail, imagine a purple light at the top of your head, where the crown chakra is located, illuminating and connecting you to the heavens. As it opens, repeat this mantra in your mind: "I have spirit coursing through my veins." After you pour your cocktail and begin to drink it down, imagine a glowing light coming from the liquid and illuminating you through your skin. As you drink, you will glow more and more, and you will connect more and more deeply with the magick of spirit.

→ → →

INVOKING SPIRIT

MOON PHASE: Full moon

OCCASION: Solo divination, small coven gathering

GLASSWARE: Martini glass

INGREDIENTS

2½ oz white rum

½ oz Luxardo® Maraschino

½ oz crème de cacao

DIRECTIONS

* Combine rum, Luxardo®
  Maraschino, crème de cacao,
  and ice into a martini shaker.

* Stir for 20 seconds.

* Hard strain into martini glass.

NONALCOHOLIC MODIFICATION

* Substitute rum with seltzer, and
  add chocolate and cherry bitters.

* Combine seltzer, bitters, and ice
  into a martini shaker.

* Stir for 20 seconds.

* Hard strain into martini glass.

The Alchemist's Tools

WHILE A PERSON TRULY ONLY NEEDS THEIR intention and energy to be a witch, there are some very helpful tools that each witch keeps in their arsenal. As alchemy is the transformation of matter, a witch will use such tools to manifest and create their will into existence. From common household items that are consecrated, to instruments created in the witch's own design, these tools are a big part of a magickal practice. Sip these cocktails to bring you closer to these tools and influence your own alchemy.

THE HEARTH

THE HOME IS A VERY SPECIAL PLACE FOR THE WITCH. As
many practitioners are solitary, this is a place of seclusion and magick in
which one can practice. There is even a category of witches, called Hearth
Witches, that practice practical magick in and around the home. This can
exist in a floor wash to bring in romance, by infusing abundance into a meal,
or by using herbs to anoint your doorway to bring in positive energy. As
"hearth" was originally coined as a term for the area around the fireplace or
stove, the name conjures up ideas of warmth. This cocktail brings the whole
energy of the hearth into you.

When I think of cinnamon, I'm brought back to my childhood at
Christmas, when my mother used to simmer cinnamon sticks on the stove,
making the whole house smell festive. Ruled by fire, cinnamon helps us
open up our root chakra, making us feel cozy and secure. Cinnamon is also
a jack-of-all-trades, aiding in the speed of a spell, as well as anything from
protection to money-drawing to love. In the home, anything is possible, and
cinnamon makes it happen.

As you stir this cocktail, breathe deep and ground yourself into the floor,
imagining the calming crackle of a fireplace. Stir clockwise, bringing in
safety, friendship, and positivity. Imagine warmth coming over you, relaxing
you. As you sip your drink, invoke the protective and comforting qualities of
the home, sinking into the knowledge that you are secure.

THE HEARTH

MOON PHASE: Waxing moon
OCCASION: Fall, potluck, dinner party
GLASSWARE: Rocks glass

INGREDIENTS

3 cinnamon sticks
2½ oz cinnamon-infused añejo tequila
1 sugar cube
3 dashes aromatic bitters
2 dashes orange bitters
Orange peel and cinnamon stick for garnish

DIRECTIONS

* Before you begin, drop a few cinnamon sticks into your bottle of añejo tequila to infuse the mixture.

* In a rocks glass, place the sugar cube at the bottom and top with bitters (and muddle).

* Pour in the tequila.

* Stir until dissolved, then add in ice and continue to stir.

* Top with your garnish.

NONALCOHOLIC MODIFICATION

* Before you begin, steep some cinnamon tea and let it chill. This will serve as a replacement for the tequila.

* In a rocks glass, place the sugar cube at the bottom and top with bitters (and muddle).

* Pour in the tea.

* Stir until dissolved, then add in ice and continue to stir.

* Top with your garnish.

THE CAULDRON

ONE OF THE MOST ON-BRAND TOOLS THAT A WITCH HAS IN
their arsenal is a cauldron. You often see witches depicted with it, stirring
in eye of newt and toe of frog. However, a cauldron is simply a safe place
to burn and mix your spell-casting tools! In fact, many practitioners use
a household pot that is blessed and used strictly for magick. Because fire
safety is important for witches that love the flame, we use a cauldron to burn
without fear of destroying our home. With this, our cauldron keeps us safe
and holds fire energy stable so that we are more focused when working with
it.

Matcha tea is known to have magickal benefits of health, longevity, and
immortality. With the swirling green, warm concoction, we are brought back
to iconic imagery of witches creating their potions. Because of the addition
of lemon, ginger, and honey, this recipe is an excellent aid in the health of a
witch, therefore amplifying its protective elements.

As you are mixing your cocktail in your cauldron, either for a single
serving or multiplied for a coven meeting, stir it clockwise and ask for
protection. As you stir, you bring in protective energies. Speak into your
mixture, for liquid has a way of transferring energy. Ask it to keep you
safe. When drinking down the finished product, envision the warmth of
fire filling you from your belly, harnessing the power of the flame, and
invigorating you to accomplish all you desire.

$\rightarrow \ \rightarrow \ \rightarrow$

THE CAULDRON

MOON PHASE: Waxing moon

OCCASION: Winter, potluck, dinner party

GLASSWARE: Mug

INGREDIENTS

1½ oz Japanese whiskey

1 oz ginger liqueur

½ oz honey syrup

½ oz lemon juice

½ tsp matcha powder

2 dashes ginger bitters

Lemon wheel for garnish

DIRECTIONS

* This recipe makes one serving, but feel free to multiply it in a cauldron for a coven gathering.

* Place all ingredients into a mug.

* Fill with hot water and stir.

* Top with your garnish.

NONALCOHOLIC MODIFICATION

* Place all ingredients into a mug, aside from the whiskey.

* Add in additional matcha to your liking.

* Fill with hot water and stir.

* Top with your garnish.

BOOK OF SHADOWS

A BOOK OF SHADOWS, OR GRIMOIRE, IS A PERSONAL
collection of spells made by the practitioner. This book is an anthology
of rituals and incantations that have worked for the witch and are kept
for when they require the same outcome. This is an extremely unique and
private compendium, because one witch's energy may not always match
another's, so in the spirit of customization, a book of shadows is essentially
a fingerprint. This drink will inspire you to create your own.

Smoke is known to clear and cleanse, evaporating negative and unwanted
energies from a given space. Because your grimoire should be a reflection of
you, smoke will allow for a clean slate from which to create. When you dry
rosemary, you can light it and use its smoke for the same clearing abilities as
you would white sage, yet rosemary is excellent for mental stimulation and
creativity.

As you are mixing your drink, sink into your power as a practicing witch.
Own your own expertise, even if it is in the ability to learn. As you light
your rosemary, ask the universe for the ability to create and practice with
ease. When placing it under the glass to fill with smoke, imagine that smoke
burning away all self-doubt and cleansing negativity. And as the smoke
rises out of the glass when you flip it to pour your cocktail, have it waft over
you, bringing you the same energy. When drinking this cocktail, begin to
envision how you can use witchcraft as an art form and begin making a list
to fill your own grimoire.

→ → →

BOOK OF SHADOWS

MOON PHASE: Full moon
OCCASION: Fall, Samhain/Halloween, coven gathering
GLASSWARE: High ball

INGREDIENTS

Dried rosemary
1½ oz mezcal
½ oz lime juice
1½ oz grapefruit juice
½ oz simple syrup

DIRECTIONS

* Before mixing your drink, light your dried rosemary on fire until it smolders.

* Turn your empty glass upside down and place it over the rosemary to capture the smoke.

* Turn the smoked glass right side up and fill with ice.

* Build the mezcal, lime juice, grapefruit juice, and simple syrup in your shaker, add ice, and shake vigorously.

* Strain into glass.

* Garnish with torched rosemary.

NONALCOHOLIC MODIFICATION

* Before mixing your drink, light your dried rosemary on fire until it smolders.

* Turn your empty glass upside down and place it over the rosemary to capture the smoke.

* Turn the smoked glass right side up and fill with ice.

* Build all other ingredients in your shaker without the mezcal, add ice, and shake vigorously.

* Strain into glass.

* Top with seltzer and garnish with torched rosemary.

SACRED SIGIL

Sigils have been used for centuries in many different practices by witches. A sacred and personally designed symbol charged with intention, a sigil is a forceful and easy-to-make tool. By taking a short-phrased intention, such as "Bring in wealth," you can craft a sigil by first crossing out all vowels, then by crossing out repeating letters, and finally by arranging the remaining letters in a pleasing design. So, for example, the previous intention would become BRNGWLTH, and using my artistic flair, I would fit those letters together in an arrangement that suits me.

Eggs are known for both their protective and fertility properties for obvious reasons. Because they are an actual source of life, and because of their hard outer shell, eggs have a feminine quality. They are also linked to intuition and are used in divinatory practices to see if negative energy is present. Sigils are most commonly employed for both protection and manifestation, so I thought egg whites to be the perfect canvas with which to paint your sigil. If you are on a vegan diet, vegan egg white substitute works just as well for this concoction.

Before mixing, think of your intention and create your sigil on a piece of paper. While dry shaking your egg white, think of your intention and hold it in your mind's eye, making it stick with every vigorous shake. As you pour your cocktail into the glass, imagine a bright, white light purifying it so that it may serve as a clean base. Once poured, use your bitters to create your sigil atop the egg white. You can use a toothpick to create cleaner lines. As you consume, visualize the power of your intention permeating your body.

→ → →

SACRED SIGIL

MOON PHASE: New to waxing moon
OCCASION: Any occasion aligned with your sigil
GLASSWARE: Coupette

INGREDIENTS

1½ oz rye whiskey
½ oz sweet vermouth
½ oz Demerara syrup
½ oz lemon juice
2 dashes aromatic bitters
1 egg white or vegan substitute
Angostura bitters for garnish

DIRECTIONS

* In your martini shaker, add in rye whiskey, sweet vermouth, Demerara syrup, lemon juice, aromatic bitters, and egg white.

* Dry shake ingredients vigorously.

* Add in ice and continue to shake.

* Double strain into a coupette.

* Drop the Angostura bitters on top of the egg white foam in the shape of your sigil and drag your toothpick across the bitters to create the magickal symbol.

NONALCOHOLIC MODIFICATION

* Replace rye whiskey and sweet vermouth with 2 oz iced tea for this recipe.

* In your martini shaker, add in iced tea, Demerara syrup, lemon juice, aromatic bitters, and egg white.

* Dry shake ingredients vigorously.

* Add in ice and continue to shake.

* Double strain into a coupette.

* Drop your bitters on top of the egg white foam in the shape of your sigil and drag your toothpick across the bitters to create the magickal symbol.

Spell
Casting

WHETHER FOR HEALING, PROTECTION, ABUN-
dance, or something else, casting a spell to manifest your
intention is one of the most appealing parts of being a
magickal practitioner. While it is not the entire sum of
the witch experience, it is a very important—and quite
fun—part of it. When casting spells, witches can deepen
their relationship with energy to bend and mold it to their
will, creating their wildest dreams in accordance with the
universe. And the beauty of a spell that didn't work? The
process of going back to the drawing board and reflecting
on what is truly your highest purpose and on what tools
will allow you to align with it best.

PURIFYING TONIC

It might sound counterintuitive to purify with alcohol, but it is quite possible with the right intention! Cleansing the body is very important in witchcraft, as we practitioners are the vessels for our magick. When we have a clear platform, we can cast our spells without any hinderance. Negativity from others, or even our own thoughts, can block our spell work, so in order to cast a spell effectively, we must routinely cleanse. Think of it as an oil change; there must be a rotation and purification of energy if we are to run smoothly and successfully. Create this cocktail with the intention of zapping away all of the negative vibes, and watch your manifestation skills grow.

Lemon and ginger are both known for their clarifying and purifying abilities. Lemon is ruled by the moon, which gives it a feminine quality and also enhances lucidity. Ginger, being a root, inspires balance and grounding, while its spicy taste gives it the ability to cleanse.

When pouring your ingredients into the shaker, imagine that all of your energy is pouring into it as well. As you shake, move your head in a counterclockwise motion to neutralize all of the negative energy that you may have within your mind or around your aura. Pour your cocktail into the glass, imagining your energy being purified by the lemon and ginger. As you drink down your tonic, envision a white light glowing within you and bringing your spirit back into balance.

PURIFYING TONIC

MOON PHASE: Waning moon
OCCASION: Celebrating the end of a project, beginning a new project, planning a goal
GLASSWARE: Highball

INGREDIENTS

1½ oz limoncello
½ oz Giffard® Ginger Liqueur
½ honey syrup
2 dashes ginger bitters
San Pellegrino® Lemon as topper
1 lemon wheel
Candied ginger

DIRECTIONS

* Add limoncello, Giffard® Ginger Liqueur, honey syrup, and ginger bitters into a shaker.

* Shake well.

* Strain over ice.

* Top with San Pellegrino Lemon.

* Add lemon wheel and candied ginger for garnish.

NONALCOHOLIC MODIFICATION

* Build soda water, lemon juice, honey syrup, and ginger bitters into a glass.

* Stir well clockwise so that the honey dissolves.

* Top with San Pellegrino Lemon.

* Add lemon wheel and candied ginger for garnish.

PROTECTIVE CIRCLE

Casting a protective circle is a step that must not be skipped in spell work. In whichever way you choose to cast it, this creates an area in which to work your magick, uninterrupted by spirits or other energetic entities. I liken this to a sterile operating room during surgery; once you enter it, you do not leave, lest you bring in outside contaminants. If you are not familiar with casting a circle, one of the most traditional ways to create it energetically is to make a physical circle with salt around you and your tools while calling out the elements at their given cardinal directions. This would be north for earth, south for fire, east for wind, west for water, and the sky for spirit. In this cocktail, you will be doing the same.

Salt in witchcraft is used as a protective barrier because of its energetic properties. It is known to cleanse, but also to cast out, negative vibrations. Its crystallized cellular makeup acts as a shield for all daily practices, making everyday table salt an important tool for the witch. So in addition to salt, I have added blueberries as an ingredient to provide an extra layer of protection. Blueberries are known to guard against psychic attacks, so this cocktail will keep you safe so that you can cast whatever spell you desire.

Before you mix this cocktail, rim the glass with the juice from a lemon wedge, creating a purified energy. Then dunk the rim into table salt to form your own mini salt circle. After it is covered in salt, call the cardinal directions of the elements as you mix up your drink. While you pour your cocktail into the glass, speak out loud what you wish to manifest, and as you drink it down, know that you are the vessel through which your spell can be carried out. After you are done and you clean your glass of the salt, thank the elements, and it is so.

→ → →

PROTECTIVE CIRCLE

MOON PHASE: Waxing moon

OCCASION: Any occasion fit for your intention, coven gathering

GLASSWARE: Collins glass

INGREDIENTS

6–8 blueberries
3 oz grapefruit juice
2 oz vodka
Additional blueberries for
garnish

DIRECTIONS

* Salt the rim of your glass.

* Muddle blueberries at the
  bottom of your martini shaker.

* Add grapefruit juice, vodka, and
  ice into your shaker.

* Shake vigorously.

* Double strain into glass over ice.

* Top with blueberries as a
  garnish.

NONALCOHOLIC MODIFICATION

* Salt the rim of your glass.

* Muddle blueberries at the
  bottom of your martini shaker.

* Add grapefruit juice and ice into
  your shaker.

* Shake vigorously.

* Double strain into glass over ice.

* Top with blueberries as a
  garnish.

MONEY MAGICK

WHO DOESN'T LOVE A GOOD MONEY SPELL? WHETHER YOU are wanting a windfall of cash or just an extra ten dollars to get you through the day, a good abundance ritual can get the juices of the universe flowing your way. By keeping your heart open, your vibration high, and your mind in a state of wealth, you can become a magnet for riches. This energetic principle has been used by witches and Law of Attraction practitioners alike. For this cocktail, remember that what you focus on grows.

The color green is an important ingredient in this cocktail, along with basil, mint, and the practice of visualization. Green is not only the color of money, but also the color of your heart chakra, which is directly linked to abundance. Basil is associated with the planet Venus, which rules love and money, and is further linked to money spells and career spells. Mint is great for money spells, but it is also associated with healing, which I find perfect for fixing a poor money mindset.

As you mix this cocktail, envision a glowing green light emanating from your heart, opening up your abundance center, and connecting you to all you desire. Keep this light glowing in your mind's eye throughout the entire mixing process. Then, imagine what money really affords you. Is it freedom? Luxury? Safety? Keep this keyword in your head when pouring into the glass. And, as you drink down this cocktail, imagine your energy being permeated with this notion. Feel more free and more secure with each sip, knowing that you are making an imprint on the universe with this emotion.

→ → →

MONEY MAGICK

MOON PHASE: New to waxing moon
OCCASION: New job, job promotion, product launch, new venture
GLASSWARE: High ball

INGREDIENTS

Mint sprig
2 oz green chili vodka
1½ oz cucumber juice
¾ oz lime juice
½ oz simple syrup
Cucumber ribbon and mint
bouquet for garnish

DIRECTIONS

* Muddle the mint sprig at the
  bottom of a shaker.

* Build the vodka, cucumber juice,
  lime juice, and simple syrup in a
  shaker with ice.

* Shake vigorously.

* Strain into a glass with ice.

* Top with garnish.

NONALCOHOLIC MODIFICATION

* Muddle the mint sprig at the
  bottom of a shaker.

* Build the cucumber juice, lime
  juice, and simple syrup in a
  shaker with ice.

* Shake vigorously.

* Strain into a glass with ice.

* Top with seltzer water.

* Finish with garnish.

LOVE POTION #9

Conjuring love is another highly coveted magickal act, and you can do so in many ways as a witch. When working with the energies of the divine feminine, you can become a sensual magnet! Love spells do have ethics, however. It is widely agreed upon that one should not cast a love spell directly onto another person. Instead, the ideal love spell simply pumps up your own energetic vibration to become its most attractive. Casting a love spell on someone specific is kind of like holding someone hostage; when you mess with the free will of a person, not only is it morally questionable, but you'll also never know if their love is real or simply a trance. When sipping this cocktail, you'll be amplifying your own romantic energy so that lovers will come knocking down your door because they want to.

Channel the magnetic energy of the goddess with the effervescence of pink champagne, amplifying self-love and confidence. Hints of rose, which have long been associated with love and the goddess Venus, bring an undertone of sensual energy, and apples highlight this cocktail as a fruit of fertility and immortality. By using all of these ingredients in one mixture, you'll be transmitting the vibration of a temptress.

As you mix your cocktail, call out to the goddess Venus to guide you in your romantic escapades. Ask her for her infinite wisdom in all things love, and allow her to sink into the vessel. Stir clockwise to invoke a loving energy. As you drink down this mixture, imagine a pink light filling you up and illuminating your heart, making your energy irresistible to your perfect match.

LOVE POTION #9

MOON PHASE: New to waxing moon
OCCASION: Weddings, bridal showers, singles night, mixers
GLASSWARE: Wineglass

INGREDIENTS

1 oz Belvoir Elderflower® and
Rose Cordial®
½ oz Cointreau®
½ oz lemon juice
Sparkling rosé as topper
2 dashes apple bitters
2 drops rose water

DIRECTIONS

* Build the cordial, Cointreau®,
  and lemon juice in a glass with
  ice.
* Stir lightly, clockwise.
* Top with sparkling rosé, apple
  bitters, and a dash of rose water.

NONALCOHOLIC MODIFICATION

* Build the cordial and lemon juice
  in a glass with ice.
* Stir lightly, clockwise.
* Top with apple bitters and a
  dash of rose water.

KEEP IT HEXY

T his cocktail eliminates all traces of a hex. A practitioner can unknowingly carry this black magick with them, being a victim of something known as the Evil Eye. Occurring after an onlooker casts a penetrating glance, the Evil Eye can create chaos. When someone is envious of the practitioner, or, more ruthlessly, wishes ill will upon them, this negative energy can cast a dark cloud over a witch, creating bad luck wherever they go. This simple hex is more common than not because most don't even know they are wielding it. Protect yourself against this powerful spell by sipping this concoction.

More readily available than the recently popularized white sage, common sage helps cleanse the aura of any trace of the Evil Eye with its purifying qualities. Though not smoked, when muddled and ingested, it can have the same cleansing abilities as its Native American counterpart. Blackberries add a protective element to your spell, being known to block negative energies with their dark color and thorny branches. Traces of black pepper not only protect, they also return the hex to the sender when this cocktail is sipped with intent.

When mixing your cocktail, imagine your luck reversing and becoming more positive. Shake vigorously, as if you are physically turning your luck around. As you pour, imagine your spirit being cleansed from any traces of the Evil Eye and being backed by all of the protection of the universe. As you drink your cocktail down, imagine negative energy dissolving on your palette and returning any ill will to the sender that consciously cast this hex.

→ → →

KEEP IT HEXY

MOON PHASE: Waning moon
OCCASION: Happy hour, self-care day
GLASSWARE: Wineglass

INGREDIENTS

3 blackberries
2 sprigs of sage
5 black peppercorns
1 oz lemon juice
1½ oz vodka
1 oz simple syrup
Soda water as topper

DIRECTIONS

* Place blackberries, sage, and black peppercorns in a shaker.
* Muddle ingredients.
* Add in ice, lemon juice, vodka, and simple syrup.
* Shake well.
* Double strain ingredients over ice.
* Top with soda water.

NONALCOHOLIC MODIFICATION

* Place blackberries, sage, and black peppercorns in a shaker.
* Muddle ingredients.
* Add in ice, lemon juice, and simple syrup.
* Shake well.
* Double strain ingredients over ice.
* Top with soda water.

Divination

DIVINATION IS THE ART OF COMBINING YOUR intuition with your tool of choice to gain insight. The witch may gain clarity on a pressing issue in the present, seek answers from the past, or even see directly into the future with this practice. Witches have divined with many different objects over the ages, from beverages to crystals to common household items. In order to divine, one must simply clear their mind and listen to the pull of their gut while extracting symbols from their given tools.

CAFEOMANCY

One way to divine is by reading coffee grounds. This practice, which interprets the figures that the coffee creates after drinking to see into the future, has been around since the time of ancient Greece. One may do this today by placing the grounds of their coffee from the coffeemaker on a napkin and reading the shape that the pile of grounds produces to see what is ahead. If drinking Greek or Turkish coffee, the bottom of the cup will be filled directly with more porous grounds, and you can interpret directly from the cup.

Coffee beans themselves have quite powerful magickal correspondences that you might think are a little on the nose. For one, coffee beans are known to have a grounding quality, and because of the caffeine, they are known to increase the speed of spell work. Because of its dark color, coffee is also excellent for banishment. And if working with deities and ancestors, coffee is also a common offering.

For this mixture, we are going to combine both spell work and divination. When mixing your cocktail, think of an intention that you would like to achieve. As you are mixing, hold it tight in your mind's eye, asking your guides to help you toward it. When pouring your drink into the glass, give thanks to your spirits for their assistance. While drinking your cocktail, keep envisioning this goal and keep your intention high. When you are finished, read the remnants of your drink on the sides of the glass. See if you can extract any figures or symbols. Whatever is on your glass is what is blocking you from your goal, and that is what you should work on before manifesting.

→ → →

CAFEOMANCY

MOON PHASE: Full moon
OCCASION: Coven gathering, friends' night, solo night in
GLASSWARE: High ball

INGREDIENTS

1 oz espresso
1 oz coffee liqueur
½ oz amaro
2 dashes aromatic bitters
½ oz simple syrup
1 oz coconut rum cream

DIRECTIONS

* Build the espresso, coffee liqueur, amaro, bitters, and simple syrup in a shaker with ice.

* Shake vigorously.

* Double strain into a glass with ice.

* Top with coconut rum cream.

NONALCOHOLIC MODIFICATION

* Build 2 oz espresso, bitters, and simple syrup in a shaker with ice.

* Shake vigorously.

* Double strain into a glass with ice.

* Top with coconut milk substitute.

CRYSTAL BALL

WE'VE OFTEN SEEN IMAGERY OF FORTUNE-TELLERS WITH beautiful headscarves and glamorous gold hoops, staring into a crystal ball and telling the querent what the future holds. While this is mostly theatrics in Hollywood, the art of divining out of crystals is a real thing! While crystal balls are often used for scrying, crystals of any shape, not just spheres, can be used to intuitively extract symbolism. By looking into the structure of the crystal—its lines, gradients, cracks, etc.—a skilled diviner can interpret what catches their eye in terms of what their client has asked of them.

In order to correctly divine with this cocktail, first we're going to make our own crystal structures! Follow the directions below to make your own rock candy, and through the ritual, you'll be able to use your intuition on the question at hand. For clarity, the main ingredient in this recipe is peppermint. Known to relieve migraines, it also energetically cleanses the mind so that one can effectively work with their intuition. Associated with the air element, this herb clears the mind and creates a clear pathway for communication.

When creating your rock candy, set the intention for clarity and answers. If you have a burning question at hand, ask it into your mixture as it creates crystals. While mixing your cocktail, imagine a white light evaporating all of the difficult thoughts in your mind and clearing a pathway for the universe to shine through. After pouring your cocktail, speak your question into the glass and place your rock candy as a garnish. As you imbibe, imagine the answers flowing into your mind, and when you are finished, see if you can interpret any symbols or shapes left on your crystal.

→ → →

CRYSTAL BALL

MOON PHASE: Full moon
OCCASION: Coven gathering, friends' night, solo night in
GLASSWARE: Martini glass

INGREDIENTS

1½ oz vodka or white rum
1 oz white chocolate liqueur
½ oz crème de cacao
½ oz peppermint schnapps
½ oz simple syrup
Rock candy garnish (see recipe below)

DIRECTIONS

* Add vodka or rum, white chocolate liqueur, crème de cacao, peppermint schnapps, simple syrup, and ice into a martini shaker.
* Shake vigorously.
* Strain into martini glass.
* Top with rock candy garnish.

NONALCOHOLIC MODIFICATION

* Add 2 oz almond milk, ½ oz chocolate syrup, and ice into a martini shaker.
* Shake vigorously.
* Strain into martini glass.
* Top with rock candy garnish.

INGREDIENTS TO MAKE YOUR OWN ROCK CANDY

2 cups water
1 cup sugar
Peppermint extract
Mason jar
A string
Clothespins

DIRECTIONS TO MAKE YOUR OWN ROCK CANDY (Note: this can take up to a week)

* Boil 2 cups of water and slowly add in your sugar.
* Add in peppermint extract.
* Let cool ten minutes.
* Pour syrup into mason jar.
* Let string hang an inch from the bottom of the jar using a clothespin to secure at the top.

WAIT AND WATCH!

SCRYING MIRROR

SCRYING IS THE ANCIENT ART OF USING REFLECTIONS TO find portals to the spirit world. Ancient Greeks, Egyptians, and Celts alike would use this art by trying to "see" through reflective liquids, such as oil. Over time, this evolved into the use of mirrors, and it is still used today! Flat surface obsidian is often used in mediumship to see into other planes and to make contact with spirits. When one softens their focus onto the mirror, over a period of time they can open their vision up to seeing shapes in a trancelike state. By receiving messages, they can then gain answers, or even see into the future.

In order to make this cocktail black in color and have the same abilities as a scrying mirror, I have chosen activated charcoal as the main ingredient. Charcoal is incredibly grounding and also cleansing, absorbing negative debris with its darkened color and vibration. Known as a detoxifier, it also has this ability on energy. In addition, it contains a strong protective element, being commonly used with table salt to create black salt in traditional magick. Because we are using this cocktail to scry, grounding, protection, and cleansing are of the utmost importance so that you may be guarded against spirits.

While you mix your cocktail, think of a question you want answers to. Ask your guides to come to you as you mix, and imagine a white circle encompassing you so that you are fully protected when scrying. Next, pour your drink into your glass and begin to soften your gaze. To properly scry, it's best to drink your cocktail in low light, but please use caution. Breathe in deeply and slowly, and then exhale, continuing into a trancelike, meditative state. Stare into your cocktail and let answers come to you, and with each sip, open yourself up more and more to receiving messages. When you are finished with your cocktail, thank your guides for protecting you and send the white circle you cast up into the heavens by visualizing it closing.

SCRYING MIRROR

MOON PHASE: Full moon
OCCASION: Coven gathering, friends' night, solo night in
GLASSWARE: Martini glass

INGREDIENTS

1 capsule activated charcoal
2 oz scotch
Maraschino liqueur, for rinse
¾ oz sweet vermouth
2 dashes aromatic bitters
Black cherry garnish

DIRECTIONS

* In separate glass, add activated charcoal capsule to 2 oz scotch.
* Stir until dissolved.
* Rinse martini glass with maraschino liqueur, pour out excess.
* Add charcoal scotch, vermouth, bitters, and ice to martini shaker.
* Shake vigorously.
* Strain into martini glass.
* Top with black cherry garnish.

NONALCOHOLIC MODIFICATION

* Replace scotch with iced black tea and maraschino liqueur with maraschino syrup.
* In separate glass, add activated charcoal capsule to 3 oz tea.
* Stir until dissolved.
* Add charcoal tea, maraschino syrup, and ice to martini shaker.
* Shake vigorously (to break up charcoal).
* Strain into martini glass.
* Top with black cherry garnish.

TASSEOGRAPHY

Similar to reading coffee grounds, tasseography is the art of reading tea leaves. In the 17th century, when Dutch merchants introduced tea to Europe through Chinese trade routes, practitioners of magick would divine through tea leaves for themselves and clients. Much like cafeomancy, the diviner would look to the arrangement of the leftover tea leaves and surmise the symbolism, interpreting the querent's fortune. You can do so today in exactly the same way, amplifying the magick by using teas that correspond to the questions you want answers from.

Deriving from China, green tea has been used in Chinese medicine for ages. Known for its aid in healing, its energizing properties, and its benefits for the heart, it's no wonder that it has found popularity in Western countries. Its green color is connected directly to the heart, as that is the color of the heart chakra, and it is known to aid in love spells. It is also known to emit a healing energy and has even been used in immortality spells.

For this cocktail, we are going to divine on matters of the heart. When shaking your cocktail, envision your heart chakra opening and receiving a loving energy from the universe. When pouring, keep in your mind's eye the intention to create abundance. Sip this drink, visualizing a green light filling you up and nourishing your heart. Continue the growth of the light. When you have finished your cocktail, look to the arrangement of the leaves on the sides of your glass. Whatever symbols you can interpret will point to your future in love.

TASSEOGRAPHY

MOON PHASE: Full moon

OCCASION: Coven gathering, friends' night, solo night in

GLASSWARE: Coupette

. . . .

INGREDIENTS

3 large basil leaves
1 lemon peel
1½ oz chilled green tea
½ oz honey syrup
1½ oz vodka
Lemon twist for garnish

DIRECTIONS

* Before mixing, boil water, and mix a 1:1 ratio of honey to hot water to make the honey syrup.

* Muddle basil leaves and lemon peel in a tin shaker.

* Build ice, green tea, honey syrup, and vodka into the tin.

* Shake vigorously.

* Strain into a glass with ice.

* Top with lemon twist (there should be remnants of basil leaves in the glass).

NONALCOHOLIC MODIFICATION

* Before mixing, boil water, and mix a 1:1 ratio of honey to hot water to make the syrup.

* Muddle basil leaves and lemon peel in a tin shaker.

* Build ice, 3 oz green tea, and honey syrup into the tin.

* Shake vigorously.

* Strain into a glass with ice.

* Top with lemon twist (there should be remnants of basil leaves in the glass).

The Tarot

ANOTHER FORM OF DIVINATION, BUT FAR TOO complex for one cocktail, is the tarot deck. Created in 15th-century Europe as a deck of playing cards with Roman Catholic imagery, the cards have been used in various practices to divine answers or tell the future. The tarot has gained a bad rap over the years, as many forms of spiritualism have, but it just goes to show that anything can be used as a magickal practice if used with intention. With 78 cards making up the entire deck, it is split into two uneven groups. The Major Arcana, which tells the story of the Fool, is comprised of 22 cards, and the remaining 56 are split into four suits, each of which symbolizes one of the four elements. From the traditional Rider-Waite deck to more artistic interpretations, every symbol, number, and color has a meaning, making it an incredibly complex system that brings new messages every time it is used.

THE FOOL

THE FIRST CARD IN THE TAROT DECK SHOWS A MAN WITH a bag tied on a string, standing over a cliff with a small dog by his feet and a white rose in his hand. The story of the Major Arcana (the titled cards of the tarot) takes us through his journey. He is full of optimism and hope, being a little naive in the best way. He is wide-eyed and bushy-tailed, and has a romantic view of the world ahead of him. He is divinely protected, pure, and excited.

Rosemary is an excellent herb for all kinds of spiritual work, but in this case, its energetic vibrations of optimism and protection are truly appropriate. Rosemary is ruled by Leo, which governs the heart, and the Fool is a very heart-centered character. He leads with it and wears it on his sleeve. It is a trait to be admired, although many seasoned cynics may call it "foolish." Known to be woven into wedding wreaths and crowns for brides, rosemary symbolizes a purity that is coveted. And just as the white dog pictured in the tarot protects the Fool, so does rosemary, being known to ward against illness and misfortune. In addition, cranberry inspires abundance, which is directly connected to the heart and is also known to increase energy! Since the Fool is said to be youthful, you can create that feeling with the properties of cranberry.

As you mix your cocktail, ask for strength and guidance from your spirits so that you may be protected in your journey. Invoke this protection and know that it is always with you. Pour the mixture into your glass, and with each sip, feel it warm your heart and open it. By drinking, allow your cynicism to wash away, leaving a new and unscathed view of the world. Embrace this optimism and write down a list of new things you'd like to accomplish, and infuse the energy of the Fool into it so that you may not be afraid and won't talk yourself out of this new and wondrous journey.

THE FOOL

MOON PHASE: New moon
OCCASION: Starting a new job, new romance, new home, new journey
GLASSWARE: Wineglass

INGREDIENTS

Sprig of rosemary
6 cranberries
1 orange peel
2 oz gin
2 dashes of cranberry bitters
(Citrus tonic as topper)
Additional rosemary sprig
for garnish

DIRECTIONS

* Muddle rosemary sprig,
  cranberries, and orange peel at
  the bottom of martini shaker.

* Build ice and gin into the tin.

* Shake vigorously.

* Double strain into glass with ice.

* Top with citrus tonic and
  cranberry bitters.

* Adorn with rosemary sprig.

NONALCOHOLIC MODIFICATION

* Muddle rosemary sprig,
  cranberries, and orange peel at
  the bottom of martini shaker.

* Build ice and a dash of water
  into the tin.

* Shake vigorously.

* Pour entire contents of tin into
  a glass.

* Top with citrus tonic and
  cranberry bitters.

* Adorn with rosemary sprig.

THE LOVERS

THE LOVERS CARD PICTURES ADAM AND EVE HOLDING hands beneath an angel backed by the sun. This card symbolizes unity and harmony, but also the balance of duality. The ruling card of the zodiac sign Gemini, this card speaks to the two halves that create a whole. The Lovers are standing in the Garden of Eden, with flames of passion behind them, showing how incredible the immersion of two into one can be. There is an omen here, however, that if there is discord, everything will fall out of balance.

Because the Lovers celebrates differences and fits them together like a puzzle piece, I have chosen two unlikely ingredients to create this cocktail. Mango, a fertile fruit with a pit, is feminine in nature and vibrates to balance, harmony, sexuality, and romance. Chili pepper is fire-ruled and masculine, igniting passion with heat. The combination of sweet and spicy goes together just like the Lovers—unique individually, but harmonious together.

When mixing this cocktail, envision balance and harmony. Invoke a sense of grounding as you pour your mixture into the glass. As you sip, write down all of the qualities that make you unique, and when you are done, begin to list complementary qualities that you may find in a mate. As you enjoy your drink, let yourself attract your perfect other half, and when you are done, it is so.

→ → →

THE LOVERS

MOON PHASE: New to full moon
OCCASION: Weddings, anniversaries, Valentine's Day, date night
GLASSWARE: High ball

INGREDIENTS

2 jalapeño rings
2 oz tequila blanco
1½ oz mango juice
½ oz lime juice
½ oz Lillet Blanc
2 dashes citrus bitters
Tajín® rim and jalapeño ring
for garnish

DIRECTIONS

* Muddle 2 jalapeño rings in a
  martini shaker.

* Build ice, tequila, mango juice,
  lime juice, Lillet, and bitters into
  the tin.

* Shake vigorously.

* Coat rim of glass with Tajín® and
  fill with ice.

* Double strain into glass.

* Top with jalapeño ring for
  garnish.

NONALCOHOLIC MODIFICATION

* Muddle 2 jalapeño rings in a
  martini shaker.

* Build ice, 4 oz mango juice, lime
  juice, and bitters into the tin.

* Shake vigorously.

* Coat rim of glass with Tajín and
  fill with ice.

* Double strain into glass.

* Top with jalapeño ring for
  garnish.

THE MAGICIAN

THE MAGICIAN CARD SPEAKS OF ALCHEMY AND manifestation. As the only card with all four suits in the symbolism (pentacles: earth; swords: air; wands: fire; cups: water), the Magician shows that with the proper tools, you can create whatever it is you desire. This card is very empowered, as the Magician is fully rooted in his confidence. A wonderful omen to receive, this card encourages resourcefulness and to take the leap when the opportunity presents itself to you.

One of the most common manifestation tools in a kitchen witch's arsenal is the bay leaf. A simple yet powerful manifestation spell is to write your desire on a bay leaf and then burn it to send it into the universe. Ruled by the sun and energetically vibrating to match the vibrations of success, it is often used in money and abundance spells, which is exactly what we're going to do with this cocktail.

Before you mix your cocktail, imagine your specific abundance desire and hold it in your mind's eye. Take your bay leaf and write a keyword or a symbol onto it. As you mix your cocktail, imagine the accomplishment of this desire, sinking into it and feeling the overwhelming joy of your achievement. Pour your cocktail in the glass and place your bay leaf on top as a garnish. As you sip down your drink, imagine your heart center glowing green and becoming a magnet for your wish. Once you are done with your drink, light your bay leaf with a lighter (carefully) and place it into the glass to release it into the universe.

→ → →

THE MAGICIAN

MOON PHASE: New moon
OCCASION: Looking to manifest abundance
GLASSWARE: High ball

INGREDIENTS

2 oz aged rum
.5 oz fernet
.5 oz bay leaf Demerara simple syrup
Cola as topper
Bay leaf for garnish

BAY LEAF SIMPLE SYRUP

2 cups Demerara sugar
1 cup boiling water
5–6 bay leaves

* Combine and steep 15–20 mins.
* Strain and cool for 2 hours.

DIRECTIONS

* Combine rum, fernet, bay leaf syrup, and ice into a martini shaker.
* Shake vigorously.
* Strain into a glass with ice.
* Top with cola and bay leaf.

NONALCOHOLIC MODIFICATION

* Combine cola and bay leaf syrup into a glass with ice.
* Stir well.
* Top with bay leaf.

THE HIGH PRIESTESS

THE HIGH PRIESTESS IS THE EPITOME OF INTUITION.
Sitting between two columns, one black and one white, she straddles the
two worlds of spirit and earth. She knows the depths of the dark and the
inspiration of the light. Her moon crown allows her connection to the
divine feminine, allowing her both learned wisdom and control of the waters
that create an intuitive knowing. She is rooted and guided in her purpose.
She is all knowing.

One of the most common herbs for enhancing intuition is lavender.
With its calming and soothing abilities, it allows the body to rest while
the mind opens to messages of the soul and spirit. A natural stress reliever,
lavender calms negative thoughts and makes way for those that matter.
The color purple is directly related to the third eye, the energy center of
intuition, and helps to develop and enhance this natural gift. Being ruled by
both Mercury, the communication planet, and Neptune, the planet of the
subconscious, this herb is used by many diviners and spiritual practitioners.

This cocktail will help you to open up to your intuition! As you shake
this cocktail, root your feet directly into the ground. Envision a purple
light emanating from your third eye, strengthening your ability to know.
Pour your cocktail into your glass, and with each sip, envision the purple
light expanding from your third eye and enveloping your entire body. As
you enjoy your cocktail with friends or alone, look around the room and
see what catches your eye. Do you see repeating numbers on the clock? A
knickknack you've forgotten about? Anything of significance? Allow your
subconscious to guide you.

THE HIGH PRIESTESS

MOON PHASE: Full moon

OCCASION: Coven gathering, friends' night

GLASSWARE: Wineglass

INGREDIENTS

2 oz lavender-infused gin

½ oz hibiscus syrup

½ oz lemon juice

½ oz simple syrup

Champagne as topper

Lavender sprig for garnish

DIRECTIONS

* Build ice, gin, hibiscus syrup, lemon juice, and simple syrup into a martini shaker.

* Shake vigorously.

* Strain into glass with ice.

* Top with champagne and lavender sprig.

NONALCOHOLIC MODIFICATION

* Replace gin with lavender tea, and champagne with seltzer water.

* Build ice, tea, hibiscus syrup, lemon juice, and simple syrup into a martini shaker.

* Shake vigorously.

* Strain into glass with ice.

* Top with seltzer and lavender sprig.

THE DEVIL

Ah, the Devil card—one that is feared by many but understood by only a few. This card symbolizes obsession and the shackles that come with it. However, with the obvious occult imagery, it also represents raw desires and black magick. As the Devil, Baphomet is a fallen angel who represents the gradients of life, be it dark, light, or the grey we all find ourselves in. The horned god is also known through folklore to be the scapegoat, or the object of blame for any negative occurrence, and in Judeo-Christian religions, what is deemed "evil." The humans depicted on the card are chained, but they are chained loosely and of their own will. They also have horns and a tail, pointing to the notion that we all have a little devil inside of us.

Dragonfruit is a sweet, thorny fruit connected to Lucifer. With its enticing taste and horned appearance, it is also linked to the deity Baphomet. Pairing this fruit with a spiced rum, symbolizing the warmth coming from the flames of the underworld, the consumer will be living in sin in no time.

When mixing this cocktail, allow yourself to feel into the movement and enjoy how your body takes shape. Use your senses to awaken the life inside of you. As you pour your concoction into your glass, celebrate your freedoms as a human being by giving thanks for being able to make and enjoy this cocktail. And as you sip, let loose a bit so that you may enjoy life's pleasures, even if it's only for one evening.

→ → →

THE DEVIL

MOON PHASE: Full moon
OCCASION: Parties, dance night, clubbing
GLASSWARE: Tiki glass

INGREDIENTS

1½ oz spiced rum
1 oz dragonfruit purée
1 oz pineapple juice
1 oz coconut milk
½ oz Demerara syrup
¾ oz banana liqueur
Melon-balled dragonfruit for garnish

DIRECTIONS

* Combine rum, puree, pineapple juice, coconut milk, syrup, and liqueur in shaker with ice.

* Shake vigorously.

* Pour into glass with ice and top with more ice.

* Finish with garnish.

NONALCOHOLIC MODIFICATION

* Increase amounts of pineapple juice, coconut milk, and puree by .5 oz.

* Combine puree, pineapple juice, coconut milk, and syrup in shaker with ice.

* Shake vigorously.

* Pour into glass with ice and top with more ice.

* Finish with garnish.

Spiritual
Connection

PART OF WITCHCRAFT IS BELIEVING IN
something bigger than yourself that connects us all. That
can exist in spirits, deities, other realms, and—at its
most basic—energy. When working with these planes, in
whichever way fits your practice, you become invigorated
by being a part of a larger power and humbled that
you are only a microcosm of it. It's a truly enlightening
experience to embrace what is more than available to the
naked eye. Belief is a very powerful thing, and whether
or not you choose to include faith into your practice, it is
always there for when you need it.

ELDER ELIXIR

THE ROLE OF AN ELDER IN A COVEN IS TO HELP WITCHLINGS
(new witches) on their path. Generally seasoned practitioners who embody
the Crone archetype, elders have a deep wisdom and understanding of the
connectivity of magick. To have faith in them is to believe that experience
equals sagacity plus power. Serving as magickal mentors, elders are active
coven members who are highly respected. As a tangible human form of the
accumulated wisdom of many generations of practitioners, they are the
picture of what is to come on a witch's path.

Invoke the spirit of the elder with rosemary, sage, and thyme. Rosemary,
as seen in previous chapters, has many magickal correspondences, but for
this particular cocktail, we use its ancient connection to remembrance.
Rosemary helps to influence future decisions with memories of past
mistakes. Sage is not only great for cleansing and clearing, but also for
infusing wisdom into your concoction. And one ingredient that cannot be
looked over in the path of a spiritual being? Courage, which is energetically
linked to thyme. This combination will have you acting in alignment with
your elders' guidance.

When stirring this drink, call out to your ancestors who have passed,
or think of someone in your life that you admire who is of significant
age. Invoke their spirit and have their energy influence yours. Ask them
a question, or just try to connect with them on an energetic level. As you
pour your drink, imagine a piece of them filling the glass and creating an
environment in which they can influence your decision making. As you
drink this cocktail down, open yourself up to their wisdom and open your
mind to the messages you may receive.

→ → →

ELDER ELIXIR

MOON PHASE: Full moon
OCCASION: Coven gathering, friends' night, solo night in
GLASSWARE: Highball

INGREDIENTS

1 oz gin
½ oz thyme liqueur
½ oz génépy
Tonic as topper
1 sprig rosemary
1 sprig sage
1 sprig thyme

NONALCOHOLIC MODIFICATIONS

* Pour tonic in a glass with ice.
* Stir lightly.
* Garnish with one sprig each of rosemary, sage, and thyme.

DIRECTIONS

* Build gin, thyme liqueur, génépy, and tonic in a glass with ice.
* Stir lightly.
* Garnish with one sprig each of rosemary, sage, and thyme.

NOTE

Thyme is energetically linked to courage, so the combination of rosemary, sage, and thyme will have you acting in alignment with your elders' guidance. However, if you do not have these herbs on hand, use what you do have and call on your ancestors for their watchful eye.

ASTRAL TRAVEL

It is said that while you dream, you can travel to different planes! If you are a practiced lucid dreamer, you can have control over what you do within your dream state and alter your subconscious so that it may have real-world outcomes. If you cannot lucid dream, however, and you find yourself going to the same places in your dreams, it is believed that you are having out-of-body experiences and being brought to the same place in the universe over and over again until you learn the message that is meant for you. Dream work consists of taking note of these places, and accompanying symbols, and surmising what they are trying to tell you.

Whether or not you are astral projecting, you can still learn a lot from your dreams! Using chamomile, an herb known to create a relaxation tea, you can slip into a slumber that is intentional. It also aids in protection and purification, which will keep you safe from other entities while traveling through different planes. Mugwort is widely known to enhance prophetic dreams, helping the imagery become more easily remembered. Its effects can be intense, however, and so it should not be consumed by pregnant women.

When mixing your cocktail, begin to think of a question you would like answers to. If you don't have one at the moment, open yourself up to any guidance that your spirits may think you need. Pour your concoction and begin to imbibe with excitement, as your dreams will tell you everything you need to know. Before bedtime, envision a white circle of light encompassing you and your bed so that you may be protected as you sleep and allow your dream state to take over. When you awake, write down any symbols you remember from your dream and research the correspondences.

ASTRAL TRAVEL

MOON PHASE: Full moon

OCCASION: Coven gathering, friends' night, solo night in

GLASSWARE: Mug

INGREDIENTS

1 teabag full of dried chamomile

4 oz hot water

2 oz bourbon whiskey

1 oz honey

2 drops of mugwort tincture

2 dashes orange bitters

Chamomile tops

DIRECTIONS

* Steep chamomile tea in 4 oz of hot water.

* Add in whiskey, honey, tincture, and bitters.

* Stir well.

* Float chamomile for garnish.

NONALCOHOLIC MODIFICATION

* Steep chamomile tea in 4 oz of hot water.

* Add in honey, tincture, and bitters.

* Stir well.

* Float chamomile for garnish.

FAERIE MAGICK

IT IS SAID THAT THE MAGICK OF THE FAE IS EARTHLY AND inspiring. An ancient and magickal race of folk, the sprites are said to enhance connectivity to nature and inspire playfulness. There are entire sects of witchcraft that worship the fae and work with faerie power in their own magick. They enjoy magick that benefits nature and others, and love to sing and make music. Work with them to enhance friendships, bring about laughter, and connect with the earth.

As faeries are nature-based beings, using flowers in this cocktail will help bring about their energy. Being directly linked to pansies, and pink pansies in particular being connected to friendship, this is the perfect combination to call about some faerie energy. The effervescence of this cocktail encourages a lively vibe and will have you and your social circle giggling like the fae.

You can make this cocktail in a big batch to share with all of your friends. As you are mixing, call to the fae to help inspire a jovial mood. Be careful, though, because faeries are known to be mischief makers. Cast a protective white light circle around you as you mix to keep trouble at bay. As you pour this cocktail for your pals, top each glass with a pink pansy. As you place the flower on the glass, imagine it glowing with a pink light and becoming charged with affectionate energy. Enjoy your night and make sure to laugh, play, sing, and dance!

→ → →

FAERIE MAGICK

MOON PHASE: New to waxing moon
OCCASION: Coven gathering, friends' night, solo night in
GLASSWARE: Wineglass

INGREDIENTS

1 oz grapefruit juice
½ oz Aperol
½ oz grapefruit liqueur
½ oz simple syrup
Champagne as topper
Pansy for garnish

DIRECTIONS

* Combine grapefruit juice, Aperol, liqueur, and simple syrup in a wineglass.

* Add in ice and stir.

* Top with champagne.

* Float a pansy for garnish.

NONALCOHOLIC MODIFICATION

* Combine 2 oz grapefruit juice and simple syrup in a wineglass.

* Add in ice and stir.

* Top with seltzer water.

* Float a pansy for garnish.

PSYCHIC MEDIUM

MEDIUMSHIP IS THE ABILITY TO COMMUNE WITH SPIRITS, human or otherwise. This gift can also be a burden, as the messages you receive tend to get too noisy to properly interpret without boundaries. When learned to channel effectively, however, this talent can provide uncovered answers to questions and guidance from beyond. As psychic abilities are a separate gift, there are few that possess the ability to gain insight from both the past and the future. This cocktail will give you a connection to the universe that will allow access to all avenues and resources, but sip with caution, as some questions are meant to be left unanswered.

As with any type of spirit work, it is essential to guard yourself accordingly. Cloves are known for their protective elements, being used in many spells to keep negative energy at bay. To increase clairvoyance, or the ability to see into the future, star anise is used so that you may pump up any natural gifts. As it is associated with both the air element (to increase communication) and the third eye chakra (to open up your intuition), it is an excellent magickal addition. To round out this cocktail, we use whiskey as a base, which is known as a common offering to ancestors.

First, cast a protective circle around you by envisioning a ring of white light surrounding you and your tools. When mixing this cocktail, call to your ancestors and spirits and ask them for guidance. Because we are using tools of both past and future, your guides will be able to see you through this journey. Pour your cocktail into your glass, and before each sip, deeply inhale and exhale, grounding yourself in the moment. While enjoying, relax into a meditative state and be receptive to thoughts and downloads that may have significance for you. As they appear in your mind's eye, write them down, and when you are finished, keep your paper somewhere you can see it. Check the paper over time to see if your answers have come to fruition.

PSYCHIC MEDIUM

MOON PHASE: Full moon

OCCASION: Coven gathering, friends' night, solo night in

GLASSWARE: Rocks glass

INGREDIENTS

Absinthe, for rinse

1 Demerara cube

2 dashes Peychaud's® Bitters

1½ oz rye whiskey

1 oz cognac

2 dashes clove bitters

Lemon peel

Star anise for garnish

NONALCOHOLIC MODIFICATIONS

* Substitute liquor with black tea.
* Combine sugar cube and bitters in glass and muddle.
* Pour tea over sugar and bitters, and stir for 5 seconds.
* Express lemon peel over cocktail.
* Finish with lemon peel and star anise garnish.

DIRECTIONS

* Rinse glass with absinthe.
* Combine sugar cube and both bitters in glass and muddle.
* In separate container, combine rye whiskey and cognac.
* Stir for 20 seconds.
* Pour over sugar and bitters, and stir for 5 seconds.
* Express lemon peel over cocktail.
* Finish with lemon peel and star anise garnish.

Cosmic Coven

MANY WITCHES (ALTHOUGH NOT ALL) USE THE energy of the planets to impact their magick. Whether it is by studying astrology, following the phases of the moon, or observing the light of the sun on the solstices, the planets and stars in our solar system have long been regarded as having powerful effects on the earth. Through these cocktails, you'll be able to ingest the power of each luminous body and carry out its influence as your own.

SOLAR POWER

THE SUN, FOR OBVIOUS REASONS, IS KIND OF A BIG DEAL.
Being the center of our universe, and giving life to our earth, it is
worshipped by many witches and pagans. It is said to be masculine in
nature, giving power with its flames. It rules the zodiac sign Leo, which is
also ruler of the heart and ego, and takes a spot in the limelight whenever
possible. As the Wheel of the Year tracks the seasons for pagans and
follows the sun's journey through its longest and shortest days, it creates an
importance on this star as the bringer of life and harvest. Inspiring many
deities, such as Amaterasu in Japan, Helios in Greece, and Huitzilopochtli,
the Aztec sun god, the sun's power is recognized across cultures.

Directly linked to the flames of the sun, orange blossom brings energy
and revitalization. As oranges are also connected to the sun's image, it in
itself is masculine and ruled by this large star. Juniper, which is the main
herb in gin, is also sun-ruled. It is both purifying and linked to the element
of fire, cleansing like the blaze of the sun with its energy.

As you mix this drink, imagine the sun directly overhead and warming
your shoulders. Envision this warmth and bask in it while you put your
mixture together and pour it into your glass. As you drink it down, feel it
warming you from within. Visualize a yellow glow right underneath your rib
cage, giving you confidence and life. Carry this energy with you throughout
your evening.

→ → →

SOLAR POWER

MOON PHASE: Any
OCCASION: Social gatherings, mixers, first date
GLASSWARE: High ball

INGREDIENTS

1½ oz gin
½ oz Aperol
1 oz orange juice
2 drops orange blossom water
½ oz simple syrup
Soda water as topper
Orange blossom for garnish

DIRECTIONS

* Combine gin, Aperol, orange juice, blossom water, and simple syrup in a shaker.
* Add in ice.
* Shake vigorously.
* Pour into a glass filled with ice.
* Top with soda water and garnish.

NONALCOHOLIC MODIFICATION

* Combine 3 oz orange juice, blossom water, and simple syrup in a shaker.
* Add in ice.
* Shake vigorously.
* Pour into a glass filled with ice.
* Top with soda water and garnish.

LUNATIONS

Many witches look to the moon for guidance, so much so that there is even a category of witches dubbed Lunar Witches! As the moon has a cycle of 29.5 days, within which it journeys through the light of the sun, each phase symbolizes a different point of growth. When the moon is new, it is at the beginning of its cycle, and this is the time to set a new intention. When the light grows, or waxes, we look for tools to build on our intention. The full moon, which is the climax of light reflected onto its surface, is a time for a return and seeing what messages are being brought to our attention. And as the light wanes, or begins to disappear, we release what didn't serve us in the attainment of our intention, and then the cycle begins again.

The moon is feminine and rules intuition, and both of the following standout ingredients will have you connecting to lunar energy in no time. Cucumber is cooling and refreshing, and ruled by the water element, it will inspire beauty, fertility, and healing. Honeydew melon, containing many seeds within it, is known to symbolize the fertile womb of the goddess. Being used directly in moon magick, it helps to amplify abundance spells in all areas, from love to money to fertility.

As you mix your cocktail, imagine the light of the moon glowing bright in the night sky. Imagine its cool silver waves washing over your shoulders like a waterfall, cleansing you and opening you up to the divine feminine. Pour this same silvery energy from your shaker into your glass, and as you consume, envision a purple light emanating from your third eye and inspiring your intuition. As you drink down your concoction, awaken the divine feminine within by placing your nondominant hand on your womb, and celebrate the lunar power within.

→ ⇥ →

LUNATIONS

MOON PHASE: Any
OCCASION: Coven gathering, friends' night, solo night in
GLASSWARE: High ball

INGREDIENTS

3 cucumber wheels
3 basil leaves
2 oz vodka
½ oz Mastiha Antica®
½ oz juiced honeydew melon
Mediterranean tonic as topper
Cucumber wheels for garnish

DIRECTIONS

* Muddle cucumbers and basil leaves in the bottom of a martini shaker.

* Combine vodka, Mastiha, melon juice, and ice.

* Shake vigorously.

* Double strain into a glass filled with ice.

* Top with tonic and garnish.

NONALCOHOLIC MODIFICATION

* Muddle cucumbers and basil leaves in the bottom of a martini shaker.

* Combine melon juice and ice.

* Shake vigorously.

* Double strain into a glass filled with ice.

* Top with tonic and garnish.

MERCURY RETROGRADE

THE PLANET OF COMMERCE AND COMMUNICATION, Mercury often gets a bad rap because it is widely infamous for its retrograde periods. Because the planet goes into its backward transit about three times a year and royally screws up our day-to-day, it hardly gets recognized for its positive qualities. Ruling both Virgo and Gemini, Mercury is the planet of networking and cerebral intelligence. Because retrogrades are the time in which, from the earth's perspective, it appears that the planet in question is moving backward in the night sky, whichever aspects the planet rules over get thrown out of whack. Living in a very tech-based world, this can prove to be messy. However, retrogrades (if given the privilege) are wonderful times for rest and introspection over characteristics they govern. This cocktail will inspire calmness and balance.

Celery is a masculine vegetable ruled by Mercury and is known to increase focus. Because of its link to the messenger planet, it is great for all things mental. In some witchcraft practices, its seeds have been used for mind control, but for the purpose of this cocktail, we're going to intend to control our own thoughts that have been thrown out of whack by this pesky transit. The cooling effects of celery will have you slowing down and reflecting on your own mercurial experience.

As you mix your cocktail, imagine a bright white light coming into your brain from the heavens and cleansing your thoughts. Pour your cocktail, and as you imbibe, open your journal and write down the answers to these three questions: How do I best communicate when I am upset? What are the things that frustrate me most? How can I slow down in response to these frustrations? Let these answers come to you as you imbibe, and allow the answers to influence your behavior through Mercury Rx.

→ → →

MERCURY RETROGRADE

MOON PHASE: Any
OCCASION: Mercury retrograde
GLASSWARE: High ball

INGREDIENTS

Celery salt
2 oz vodka
1 oz celery juice
4 oz Bloody Mary mix
Celery for garnish

DIRECTIONS

* Rim your glass with celery salt.
* Add vodka, celery juice, and Bloody Mary mix into the glass with ice.
* Stir well.
* Top with celery garnish.

NONALCOHOLIC MODIFICATION

* Rim your glass with celery salt.
* Add 2 oz celery juice and Bloody Mary mix into the glass with ice.
* Stir well.
* Top with celery garnish.

BIRTH OF VENUS

VENUS IS THE PLANET OF LOVE AND MONEY. AS THE planet that rules luxury and decadence, she is much like the Empress of the tarot: lush and fertile. Ruling both Taurus and Libra, this goddess planet inspires the arts. The Roman Venus (of the same name) and her Greek counterpart, Aphrodite, are deities that represent all of the factors governed by this planet, such as a coveted beauty. I imagine Venus as being fanned by palm leaves in a daybed and being fed grapes by strong, scantily clad men as she lounges in abundance. This cocktail will awaken feelings of the same extravagance.

In order to convey the true meaning of Venus, I had to compile two of the most sweet and sensual flavors into one cocktail. Vanilla has been used as an aphrodisiac. Being ruled by Venus and the water element, it is no wonder it is seen as being connected to the divine feminine. Warm, inviting, and attractive, vanilla has the regal elements of the goddess, but its simplicity and accessibility allow it to be layered with whichever style and flavor the practitioner chooses. Strawberry is a fruit of love and luxury, and promotes fertility. Again, ruled by Venus, its rosy color links it directly to the sacral chakra, awakening the sexual nature.

When mixing this cocktail, call out to Venus for her glamorous essence and invoke the spirit of beauty. With each ingredient added, sink into this feeling. As you pour into your glass, awaken your senses by smelling the notes of the cocktail and drinking it slowly. When imbibing, make a list of the ways you can treat yourself this week and allow yourself the freedom to pamper. If you're feeling extra Venusian, give yourself a face mask or pedicure as you sip.

→ → →

BIRTH OF VENUS

MOON PHASE: New to full moon
OCCASION: Spring, date night, self-care night
GLASSWARE: High ball

INGREDIENTS

1 strawberry
1½ oz vanilla vodka
½ oz elderflower liqueur
2½ oz almond milk
½ oz simple syrup
Strawberry top for garnish

DIRECTIONS

* Muddle whole strawberry at the bottom of a martini shaker.

* Add vanilla vodka, elderflower liqueur, almond milk, simple syrup, and ice.

* Shake vigorously.

* Double strain into a glass with ice.

* Top with strawberry garnish.

NONALCOHOLIC MODIFICATION

* Muddle whole strawberry at the bottom of a martini shaker.

* Add 3 oz almond milk, a dash of vanilla extract, and ice.

* Add in the simple syrup.

* Shake vigorously.

* Double strain into a glass with ice.

* Top with strawberry garnish.

Color
Magick

DID YOU KNOW THAT EVEN A HUE CAN CARRY a magickal quality? Colors all vibrate to different frequencies and help us to bring in our intention. They have many different uses, from influencing intentional outfits, to makeup, and even to cocktails! For this particular section, I have divided several powerful shades into the energy sources that they influence so that you may paint your life with the colors of the rainbow! Imbibe in Technicolor with these powerful potions.

THIRD EYE

Purple is said to influence intuition. As associated with the third eye chakra in the Indian traditions and your Yesod (stomach) in Kabbalah, purple energizes perceptivity. As it is also the color of royalty and lavish living, it also creates a regal spirit. Burning a purple candle during divination can help to open you up to premonitions, and wearing purple can make you feel like a queen (or king!) who leads with their gut.

Black currants are commonly paired with champagne to create a Kir Royale, which serves as the inspiration for this cocktail! Black currants not only create a purple hue when crushed, they also add an element of protection that is so crucial when working with magick. Also associated with abundance spell work, the black currant adds to the regality of the purple energy. The effervescence of this drink adds an element of majesty to your world.

When mixing this drink, imagine a purple light glowing from your third eye and opening up your intuition. Imagine that light creating an imprint on your intuition, slowly traveling down to your gut and connecting the two places of intuitive knowing. As you pour your drink, imagine this light enveloping you like a royal cape, cascading down and knighting you with abundance. While sipping this cocktail, affirm that you are an actual queen, and sip with the confidence it takes to rule your queendom.

THIRD EYE

MOON PHASE: Full moon
OCCASION: Coven gathering, friends' night, solo night in
GLASSWARE: Rocks glass

INGREDIENTS

6–8 currants
½ oz crème de mûre
2 oz gin
1 oz lemon juice
½ oz simple syrup
Currants and lemon wheel for garnish

DIRECTIONS

* Muddle currants with crème de mûre at the bottom of a martini shaker.
* Combine gin, lemon juice, and simple syrup into a separate shaker.
* Shake vigorously.
* Add ice over muddled mixture, then add shaken mixture over ice.
* Swizzle to create a blended effect.
* Top with currant and lemon wheel garnish.

NONALCOHOLIC MODIFICATIONS

* Muddle currants at the bottom of a martini shaker.
* Combine lemon juice and simple syrup.
* Shake vigorously.
* Strain into glass with ice.
* Add seltzer water.
* Top with currant and lemon wheel garnish.

LAPIS LAZULI

LAPIS LAZULI IS A BLUE STONE OF FRIENDSHIP AND authentic expression. Connected with the throat chakra, which is also the color blue, lapis lazuli promotes communication from the heart. In order to have strong friendships, you must be able to speak directly and openly, and that is what this stone is all about. The color blue can be associated with both air and water, air ruling the ability to speak and water ruling the feelings that motivate speech.

In order to get this drink the perfect hue, blue spirulina powder is used to intensify the shade. Created from two types of algae, blue spirulina carries the element of water with it from the depths of the ocean. This will help promote access to emotion. Pineapple, which inspires strength, vigor, and courage, will allow you to speak these emotions confidently into existence, empowering you to reveal your truth and stand by it.

As you mix this cocktail, imagine a blue light emanating from your throat. The blue light should feel cooling, loosening your vocal chords and massaging into your heart. When you pour your cocktail, think of what has been on your mind, and with each sip, think of a tactful and meaningful way to bring it up. By the end of your drink, you should have the courage to bring it up.

→ → →

LAPIS LAZULI

MOON PHASE: Full moon
OCCASION: Friends' night, mixer, networking event
GLASSWARE: High ball

INGREDIENTS

1½ oz white rum
1 oz coconut rum cream
½ oz Bénédictine
1 oz lime juice
2 oz pineapple juice
1 oz simple syrup
1 egg white or vegan substitute
½ capsule blue spirulina
Pineapple leaf for garnish

DIRECTIONS

* Combine rum, rum cream, Bénédictine, lime juice, pineapple juice, (egg white) and simple syrup into a shaker with no ice.

* Shake vigorously.

* Add ice and shake again.

* Strain into glass.

* Top with pineapple leaf garnish.

NONALCOHOLIC MODIFICATIONS

* Replace rum and rum cream with 2½ oz of almond milk.

* Combine almond milk, lime juice, pineapple juice, and simple syrup into a shaker with no ice.

* Shake vigorously.

* Add ice and shake again.

* Strain into glass.

* Top with pineapple leaf garnish.

ABUNDANT AURA

THE COLOR GREEN IS MY FAVORITE, AS IT IS ASSOCIATED with the heart chakra, with money, and with overall abundance. This color helps to open your love and compassion center, which leads to financial gain when used in tandem with strong boundaries. A heart chakra that is perfectly balanced will say "yes" to the right things and "no" to the wrong things. Too open, and one can become dependent on outside forces. Too closed? One can become shut into their own prison and feel closed off from life's pleasures. This cocktail will help to keep you in balance so all of the abundance in the world may shower over you.

The color green is reached by using a French liqueur, Green Chartreuse. An investment liquor, this will already open up your abundance center by purchasing something luxurious. The kiwi fruit is Venus-ruled and feminine, with seeds in the belly just as a fertile goddess. The green color directly influences abundance, and its tart flavor inspires well-defined boundaries. Used in love and money spells alike, the kiwi will elevate the magick of this cocktail.

As you mix your drink, imagine a green light emanating from your heart's center. Open up this light and let it wash over you, inspiring your ability to love, be loved, to have money, and to hold money. As you pour your cocktail, feel the energy of having all you desire hug you with excitement, as if you already have it. With each sip, let abundance flow down your throat and warm your heart, making you a magnet for all that you desire.

→ → →

ABUNDANT AURA

MOON PHASE: New moon
OCCASION: Manifesting a new job, new love
GLASSWARE: High ball

INGREDIENTS

2 skinless kiwi slices
2 oz gin
¼ oz lime juice
¼ oz dry curaçao
¼ oz Green Chartreuse
Tonic as topper
Kiwi slice for garnish

DIRECTIONS

* Muddle kiwi slices at the bottom of a martini shaker.
* Add gin, lime juice, dry curaçao, chartreuse, and ice.
* Shake vigorously.
* Double strain into a glass with ice.
* Top with tonic and kiwi slice.

NONALCOHOLIC MODIFICATION

* Muddle kiwi slices at the bottom of a martini shaker.
* Add lime juice, ½ oz of simple syrup, and ice.
* Shake vigorously.
* Double strain into a glass with ice.
* Top with tonic and kiwi slice.

THE EGO

Yellow is the color of joy, happiness, and friendship. And although the ego gets a bad wrap, it's an essential part of our psyche that shouldn't be shamed. Leo, the sign of the lion, rules the heart and the ego, and Leo itself is ruled by the sun. The ego is essentially the same as the sun, as it is a source of outward light that illuminates and allows life to grow. While it can burn you if you're not careful, it is the lens through which your subconscious is interpreted, without which we would be swimming in the depths with no direction. Connected to our solar plexus chakra, the ego gives life to confidence and joy.

Turmeric's golden color is reminiscent of the sun's rays and our solar plexus. Derived from a root, it helps to promote grounding, which is excellent when working with the ego (so you don't get too in your head.) With its antioxidant and anti-inflammatory abilities, it is associated with healing, which allows the ego to bounce back when bruised.

When mixing your cocktail, imagine the sun's rays washing over your shoulders, warming you, and illuminating you. As you sink into this kind warmth, allow it to open up your solar plexus chakra, creating a yellow glow from right under your rib cage. Ask this light to empower you and give you confidence. Pour your cocktail and, for each sip, list one thing that you are gifted at or that makes you unique.

THE EGO

MOON PHASE: Any
OCCASION: Social gathering, first date, singles night
GLASSWARE: High ball

....

INGREDIENTS

Honey, chili salt, turmeric for rim
1½ oz mezcal
½ oz chili liqueur
1½ oz orange juice
1 oz honey/turmeric syrup

HONEY/TURMERIC SYRUP

1 cup boiling water
1 cup honey
1 tbsp turmeric

* Stir until dissolved.
* Let cool 2+ hours.

DIRECTIONS

* Rim glass with honey, chili salt, and turmeric.
* Combine mezcal, chili liqueur, orange juice, honey/turmeric syrup, and ice into a shaker.
* Shake vigorously.
* Strain into glass.
* Top with more ice if needed.

NONALCOHOLIC MODIFICATIONS

* Rim glass with honey, chili salt, and turmeric.
* Combine orange juice, honey/turmeric syrup, and ice into a shaker.
* Shake vigorously.
* Strain into glass.
* Top with seltzer water.

SACRAL SIP

YOUR SACRAL CHAKRA IS YOUR SEXUAL ENERGY CENTER.
Located in your pelvic region, this source powers passion, creativity, and
sensuality. It is connected to the color orange and leads to inspiration and
expression through action. Symbolically linked to fire in a masculine quality,
this color awakens assertiveness to complete the tasks that will carry out
your vision. It awakens how you interact with others and empowers your
ability to choose by going with what feels right and steering clear from what
doesn't.

Blood orange promotes joy and optimism, and inspires creativity, but it
also represents life, as its juice and name represent the blood that courses
through our bodies. Arousal occurs when we have extra blood flowing into
our nether regions, which awakens a spiritual experience inside of us. Blood
orange mimics that in nature's form. By using its juice in this concoction, we
are connecting with our sexual energy and using it to power us forward.

When mixing this cocktail, imagine your sacral chakra glowing a deep
orange. Imagine it warming you and exciting you. As you pour your cocktail,
connect with this energy center and feel it awaken your creativity. As you
drink your cocktail, take the time to do something creative, such as painting,
writing poetry, or even creating a mood board on Pinterest!

SACRAL SIP

MOON PHASE: Full moon
OCCASION: Date night, creative projects
GLASSWARE: Coupette

INGREDIENTS

2 oz rye whiskey
1 oz blood orange juice
½ oz simple syrup
½ oz bianco vermouth
2 dashes aromatic bitters
1 egg white (substitute with vegan
alternative if needed)
2 dashes orange bitters
Dried blood orange wheel

DIRECTIONS

* Add rye whiskey, blood orange
  juice, simple syrup, vermouth,
  both bitters, and egg white in a
  martini shaker.

* Shake vigorously without ice.

* Add ice and shake vigorously
  again.

* Strain into glass.

* Top with dried blood orange
  wheel.

NONALCOHOLIC MODIFICATION

* Substitute rye with iced black tea.

* Add black tea, blood orange juice,
  simple syrup, bitters, and egg
  white in a martini shaker.

* Shake vigorously without ice.

* Add ice and shake vigorously
  again.

* Strain into glass.

* Top with dried blood orange
  wheel.

BLOODSTONE

The deep, sensual color of red is connected to both passion and grounding. The combination of fire and earth in this particular shade of red connects with the root chakra, which governs our personal sense of safety. At the base of our spine and the center of our body, this chakra balances us and influences our survival mechanisms. Our basic needs are asked to be nurtured in this source of energy, and the color red gives us the ambition to meet them.

To accomplish the earthy red hue governed by the root chakra, one must use beets, a root vegetable. Because they grow in the soil, beets contain a very grounding energy. The beet's shade, in turn, gives us the same passion as its associated chakra. Beets contain incredible healing powers, both magickally and medicinally, as they are known to stimulate red blood cell production, decrease inflammation, and help clean the liver. Beets also connect you to your bloodline, where you may inherit internalized feelings of safety and abundance.

As you mix your cocktail, imagine the base of your spine glowing a deep red, connecting you to the ground beneath you. Imagine roots growing from the soles of your feet, fusing you with the earth. When pouring this cocktail, affirm that you are safe and ask you ancestors to keep you safe. Connect with them as you drink each sip of this cocktail. Continue holding this grounding energy for as long as you need it.

BLOODSTONE

MOON PHASE: Any

OCCASION: Coven gathering, friends' night, solo night in

GLASSWARE: Martini glass

INGREDIENTS

1½ oz gin

1 oz beet juice

¾ oz lemon juice

¾ oz honey syrup

Beet round and/or leaf for garnish

DIRECTIONS

* Add gin, beet juice, lemon juice, honey syrup, and ice into martini shaker.

* Shake vigorously.

* Strain into martini glass.

* Add beet round to side of glass for garnish, or float a beet leaf.

NONALCOHOLIC MODIFICATION

* Add 2 oz beet juice, lemon juice, honey syrup, and ice into martini shaker.

* Shake vigorously.

* Strain into martini glass.

* Add beet round to side of glass for garnish, or float a beet leaf.

Index

continued

Lavender, and intuition-enhancing properties, 90

Law of Attraction practitioners, and riches, 59

Leaves, reading, 78

Lemon
as cold remedy, 9
and health of a witch, 43
clarifying and purifying abilities of, 54, 56

Lemongrass, and the element of air, 32

Leo
and rosemary, 82
as ruler of hearth and ego, 132
and the Sun, 110

Love Portion # 9 (cocktail), 62–63

Lovers, the (cocktail), 85–87

M

Magician, the (cocktail), 88–89

Maiden, the (cocktail), 14–16

Major Arcana, 80

Mango, vibration energy of, 85

Matcha tea, 43

Mediumship, 105

Mercury
and lavender, 90
as planet of commerce and communication, 116

Mezcal, use in celebrations, 11

Mint, and healing, 59

Money Magick (cocktail), 59–61

Moon, and intuition, 113

Mother, the (cocktail), 16–18

Mugwort, enhancing prophetic dreams with, 100

N

Neptune, and lavender, 90

O

Obsidian
use in mediumship, 75
warding off negative energy with, 7

Orange blossom, and energy and revitalization, 110

P

Pansies, 102

Peach, linkage to the maiden, 20

Pentacle
and the Magician card, 86
and symbolic representation of elements, 26

Peppermint, divining with, 72

Persephone (Greek goddess), 14

Pineapple
properties of, 126
and strength, vigor, and courage, 126

Pink pansies, 102

Pomegranate, association with fertility, 14

Prophetic dreams, enhancing dreams with, 100

Protective Circle (cocktail), 56–58

Psychic attacks, protection against, 56

Purifying Tonic (cocktail), 55–56

Purple
and crown chakra, 36
and intuition, 124
link to the third eye, 90, 113

R

Red, connection to passion and grounding, 136

Relaxation tea, 100

Retrograde periods of Mercury, 116

Rock candy, 72–74

Root chakra
and cinnamon, 41
and the color red, 136

Roots of the Earth (cocktail), 34–35

Rosemary
and ancient connection to remembrance, 99
drying, 46
energetic vibrations of optimism and protection, 82
sage, and spirit of coven elder, 97
using as clearing agent, 46
warding off sickness with, 8

Rum
spiced, and dragonfruit, 92
and symbolization of crone, 20
in Vodou and Santeria, 11

S

Sacral Sip (cocktail), 134–136

Sacred Sigil (cocktail), 49–51

About the Authors

SHAWN ENGEL IS THE BRAND strategist and spiritual mentor behind *Witchy Wisdoms*. She is the author of *Cosmopolitan's Love Spells* (Sterling) and *Power of Hex* (Chicago Review Press). She has over 100,000 followers on social media, spanning Instagram, TikTok, and Twitter under the handle @witchywisdoms.

STEVEN NICHOLS IS AN AWARD-winning bartender and cocktail curator working in Jersey City, NJ. His cocktails have been featured in multiple publications, including *Forbes*. He showcases his work on Instagram @shake_n_swizzle.